YOUNG PEOPLE'S INTRODUCTION TO BUDDHISM

A Sangha Award Studybook for Shin Buddhist Scouts

by
Rev. Phillipp Karl Eidmann

BUDDHIST CHURCHES OF AMERICA

NATIONAL HEADQUARTERS
1710 OCTAVIA STREET
San Francisco, California 94109

I

PREFACE

This book has primarily been prepared to help Buddhist Boy Scouts to study for the Sangha Award. However, it is a text that can be utilized by all young Buddhists. Scouts will work with their minister or religious counselor when working on the Sangha Award program. Other young people may work with their instructors or advisors in their respective sessions.

As you work through the book, you may find some parts harder than others. Each section has questions. The answers are to be written out, but your counselor may want to discuss the answers with you instead. In each section, there are new words to learn. Nothing in your education is more important than learning new words. Words are the tools of thinking. The more words you know, the more clearly you are able to think. Learn the new words in each section. Study them. Make them your own.

When you sit down to work on this book, be sure to have a dictionary at hand. The *Thorndike-Barnhart High School Dictionary* is a very good single-volume dictionary; or the two-volume *World Book Dictionary* would be a great help. Look up the meanings of words you don't know.

Look at the title of the section you are going to read; then look at the questions carefully. Next read the section rapidly. Look again at the questions and read the section through again, looking up words you may not know. Then begin to write out the answers to the questions as you read the section for the third time. After you have written out all the answers quickly skim through the chapter for the fourth time. Then answer the questions aloud to yourself.

Your written answers should be in **complete sentences.** Then there is no need to copy the questions. The answer will serve as a kind of outline to the section. Keep the answers as short as possible. Review your answers from time to time.

But, remember that however much you know **about** Buddhism, the important thing is to **know the Buddha in your own heart.**

The last part of this text is a collection of scriptures, simplified for readability, so that the young people can begin to get used to the reading of this type of material. The original style, wording, and content is preserved as far as practical.

The Rev. Philipp K. Eidmann
Buddhist Fellowship of Sunnyvale
814 Dartshire Way
Sunnyvale, California 94087

FOREWORD

An urgent need for a text on Buddhism suitable for the young people has long been felt in the Buddhist Churches of America circles. The compilation of this text by the Reverend Philipp K. Eidmann of the Buddhist Fellowship of Sunnyvale has fulfilled this long cherished need.

This book is written on a reading level of the young people and in an easily understandable language. The writer's contemporary approach to the heart of Buddhism makes this text a very practical and useful book for all young people.

Although the text was primarily written for instruction in the Boy Scout Sangha Award program, it is most suitable for use in the upper Sunday School classes and in other youth's study sessions. Particularly, the questions listed at the end of each chapter will prove most helpful to the students as well as the instructors.

The Buddhist Churches of America and the National Buddhist Committee on Scouting are most grateful to the Rev. Philipp K. Eidmann for his devoted effort in the compilation of this book.

Metta,
Rev. Hogen Fujimoto
National Director,
BCA Youth Department
Member,
Committee on Scouting

TABLE OF CONTENTS

PART I

PART II

INTRODUCTION

In olden days army scouts led the way as the army advanced. Indian scouts led the braves in war and peace. Scouts were the path-finders. They were the guides. They did not think of themselves alone. They thought of those who followed them. Everywhere scouts had to see things as they really were. A peaceful looking valley might hide an ambush, and it was the scouts' job to see things as they really were. The good scout could never be misled by appearances. This, too, is what Buddhism teaches us: never be misled by appearances.

The Buddhist religion teaches that men are too easily misled about life. We do not see things as they really are. We do not see that ambushes lie in our path. But Buddhism shows us how to see the ambushes that lie before us, and it tells us how to avoid them. Moreover, not only are we able to avoid these ambushes ourselves, but we can help others to avoid them, too. So, in a real sense, Buddhism teaches men how to be real scouts!

The duty of Buddhist scouts is to lead themselves through life wisely and well, and to help others, also, to find happiness and joy in life, for joy and happiness are not found everywhere. They must be scouted out, just as the scouts of the Redman searched out the buffalo which were so important to their tribes. The Buddhist scout trains himself to read the signs of life, and then he guides his fellow man to happiness and joy.

The real Buddhist scout is called a bodhisattva. This word means a seeker of Enlightenment. Enlightenment means to be fully awake, so that the seeker sees things as they really are. The bodhisattva wants to be fully awake as he passes through life; he is not satisfied to be half asleep. Like the army scout or the Indian scout, the bodhisattva reads signs as he goes through life, and he knows what dangers he will face, as well as what has happened before he came along.

The great guide, for the Buddhist scout, is Gautama, the Buddha. He was the first explorer to open the trail to us; he is the fully awakened guide and teacher.

Questions (the answers are to be written out)

1. What is the job of a scout? 2. What can mislead a scout? 3. About what are men easily misled? 4. What does Buddhism teach men to be? 5. What is the duty of Buddhist scouts? 6. What must be scouted out like buffalo? 7. What does the word bodhisattva mean? 8. What does the word Enlightenment mean? 9. What does the bodhisattva want? 10. What does the bodhisattva know? 11. Who is the first explorer to open a trail through life for us? 12. Who is the fully awakened guide and teacher?

OF DIFFICULT THINGS

"But Buddism is so hard to understand!" People say this often, but is it really so? Long ago an Indian monk came to China. The Emperor called him to the palace and asked what Buddha's teaching was.

The monk replied, "Cease from evil, do good, make your own heart pure: this is the teaching of the Buddhas."

"But," countered the Emperor, "any child of six or seven knows as much. There is nothing so remarkable about this."

"Yes," replied the Indian, "any child of six or seven knows as much, but even a man of sixty or seventy finds it difficult to practice this."

"The Buddha's teaching is not so difficult to understand, but it is difficult to practice in our lives. Only when we are trying to live the Buddha's teaching can we truly be called Buddhists."

In order to practice Buddha's teaching, we must first study and understand it. Here many people become discouraged. "Buddhist books are too difficult!" "Buddhist writers use too many strange words!" We hear a thousand kinds of complaints.

But, does a fourth grader say: "My geography book is too hard because it has too many strange words! I cannot learn it." No, he sits down and learns the new words which appear in his geography book. The same is true with science, art, literature: we learn their vocabulary, and then we understand what they are about.

So, too, we must learn the words that Buddhism uses: then we will understand what the Buddha teaches. We must learn a few new words, and we must think about the meaning of some old ones. But this is not too difficult a task in the end, and the rewards are great.

Buddhism is not really difficult to understand, if we are not too lazy to try. A scout, a seeker for Enlightenment, cannot be too lazy to try. He must strive for understanding.

Questions (to be answered in writing)

1. What do many people say about Buddhism? 2. What did one Indian monk say was the teaching of the Buddhas? 3. What did the Chinese Emperor think of the Indian's verse? 4. What reply did the monk make to the Emperor's criticism? 5. What is difficult about Buddha's teachings? 6. When can we call ourselves Buddhists? 7. What two things must we do before we can practice Buddhism? 8. Why do people become discouraged when they start to study Buddhism? 9. What must we learn when we start to study a new subject? 10. How can we understand what the Buddha teaches? 11. For what must a scout strive?

THE BUDDHA

In ancient times, in the foothills of the Himalayas, lay the Sakya nation. It was ruled by the wise and just King Suddhodana. One holiday season, Maya, his fair queen, dreamed that a great white elephant had entered her side, and she knew that she was about to have a child. When she told this to her royal husband, he, his court, and the whole nation rejoiced exceedingly.

When the child's birth was near, Maya set out for her parents home, for it was the custom that a child be born in the home of its mother's parents. Maya's time came when she and her retinue were passing the park of Lumbini. There, amid the majesty of nature, she gave birth to a son, who was named Siddhartha. Gladness filled the whole Sakya nation. But within eight days, the Queen died, and sorrow, too, showed itself in the world.

Siddhartha's father, Suddhodana, saw that the child was educated in all the learning of ancient India. Siddhartha excelled in literature, in science, and, though he took no special interest in them, in the military arts. But, in all things Siddhartha was sheltered by his father, the king, so the royal child knew only the pleasures of life. It was hoped the prince would grow up to be a great and just king.

When Siddhartha reached manhood, his father urged him to marry so that the royal house would continue. Siddhartha sought a wife in a neighboring kingdom, and his suit was successful when the beautiful Yasodhara agreed to be his wife. Their union was blessed in time by a son who was named Rahula.

It chanced that one day Siddhartha saw, in a public park, a poor man and asked what this was, for he had been sheltered against every unpleasantry of life. Later he saw a sick man, an old man, and finally a dead man. Thus Siddhartha came first to know that life was not all pleasant. He was now disturbed at the problems of life. He thought much about them. Finally he left his palace one night and set out to learn why life was filled with suffering and anxiety.

For six years, the prince tried to solve the problems of life. He asked help of all the great spiritual leaders and teachers of his time, but they could not satisfy him; they could not answer his questions. He practiced various ascetic disciplines. But these were fruitless. At last he seated himself beneath a tree. He promised himself that he would not leave until he had solved his problems. That night, he attained to Enlightenment. He awakened to the truth, and fully understood the cause of suffering and its cure.

Siddhartha had become now the Buddha, the Awakened

One. After a short time, the Buddha set out for Benares. Here he met five friends from the days of his asceticism. To them he preached his first sermon, which set in motion the Wheel of the Law of truth. He told them that spiritual freedom lies in walking a middle path between asceticism on one side and giving in to lust and greed on the other. The five understood his message and became his disciples.

For many years, the Buddha travelled about India. He taught all who would listen to his message. He gained many lay-followers. Many men and women joined his Order as monks and nuns. At last in his eightieth year, the Buddha was travelling with a band of disciples; they came to the shores of the Hiransvati river. Here the Buddha became ill. Lying between two sala trees, the Buddha preached his last sermon to the disciples who were with him. Then, after urging them to strive to overcome the passions, he passed on into complete and final Nirvana.

Questions (to be answered in writing)

1. Who was Siddhartha's father? 2. Of what country was he king? 3. Who was Siddhartha's mother? 4. At the time of the Conception, of what did she dream? 5. Why did Maya set out for her home? 6. What does the word "retinue" mean? 7. In what park was Siddhartha born? 8. When did Maya die? 9. How was Siddhartha educated? 10. What was the hope for Siddhartha? 11. Why did Suddhodana want Siddhartha to marry? 12. Whom did Siddhartha marry? 13. Who was the child of Siddhartha? 14. What four sights led Siddhartha to know that there is suffering in the world? 15. What did Siddhartha do to solve his problems about suffering and anxiety? 16. For how long did Siddhartha try to solve his problems? 17. To whom did he put questions about suffering and anxiety? 18. What does the word "ascetic" mean? 19. What is a "discipline"? 20. What did Siddhartha do when he sat down beneath a tree? 21. What does the word "enlightenment" mean? 22. Where did the Buddha go after his enlighten-

ment? 23. Whom did he meet there? 24. What did the Buddha's first sermon say?

IMPERMANENCE

When we look about us, we see life is full of changes. A child is born. He grows and finally becomes an adult. He changes from a young man into an old man. We see the trees of the forests; we see the flowers of the fields. They grow, go to seed, and die. The seeds sprout, plants grow, wither and die.

When we look at stone, or a hard metal like iron, we think it will last for ever. Yet, rust destroys iron rapidly. Wind, and water and weather slowly wear away the stone until it turns to grains of sand, and then dust.

"All created things are impermanent," said the Dhammapada. Impermanence is a basic teaching of Buddhism. Everything is impermanent. Everything is constantly changing. Everything is transient.

When we look at life through a microscope, we can often see the very changes that are going on. We can see that what seems permanent is actually impermanent. Modern science has shown that all things are made of atoms, but these atoms, too, are constantly changing. Electrons and neutrons are whirling about within each atom. Even the hardest stone is made up of constantly moving atoms.

Change, then, is all about us, but we look for permanency. We desire freedom from change. Impermanency makes us uneasy. We try to make patterns and schedules in our lives. We go to bed or get up at the same time every day. We eat at the same time. We make rules to live by.

When our rules are changed we are annoyed. When other people interfere with our patterns of life, we are frustrated. Man longs for an eternal, unchanging soul. He desires a permanent, ever-lasting heaven. This longing for permanency brings to man suffering and sorrow. For compounded, created things cannot be made lasting and changeless.

Impermanency, transiency, change is the very essence of life. Every compounded thing is impermanent. Man's search for changelessness is at the root of his anxiety and worry. Man's attachment or grasping towards permanence affects his whole being.

Questions (to be answered in writing)

1. What are five examples of change in the world? 2. What does "impermanent" mean? 3. What does "transient" mean? 4. Are atoms permanent, unchanging "things"? (TO ANSWER THIS, SEE AN ENCYCLOPEDIA). 5. How do human beings try to create unchanging lives? 6. What is the result of longing for permanency?

SOULLESSNESS

The world about us seems solid and real. A stone, a piece of furniture, the ground below our feet, all seem hard and solid.

But science has proved that things are not what they seem! Our world is made up of atoms which are always whirling and turning. The parts of an atom, too, are constantly in motion.

If these parts of the atom were as big as the earth, still the space between them would be as great as the space between the earth and the stars.

The atoms that make up a stone, a piece of furniture, the ground beneath our feet, are mostly empty space.

All the atoms in the whole universe are constantly changing, impermanent, and fleeting. They have no permanent and unchanging substance in them. The atoms have no eternal nature in them.

We human beings are like this, too. Man's body and mind

are ever changing. Science can find no permanent and lasting nature in man. It can find no eternal soul.

Belief in a soul, however, is a very old superstition. Most of the religions have insisted that man has a soul which he must "save."

Buddhism, however, says that man has no soul. "All existent things have no real substance. He who knows this puts an end to suffering."

When we look at world history, we see the great truth of this fundamental point of Buddhism. The belief in a lasting soul, or ego, or spirit, has been the cause of much of the world's suffering. It has led to selfishness and tyranny.

The idea of a soul has led to religious wars and to the conquest and killing of non-believers. It makes men feel separated from their neighbors. It makes people think they are superior to their fellowmen.

The idea of a soul, or selfhood, is the basis and cause of desire, craving, thirst, and clinging to existence. Therefore it is the chief cause of all the suffering, anxiety, and fear that is part of life.

Knowing there is no soul, Buddhists can be free of personal desire, and thereby they can become free of suffering.

In the midst of hate, sorrow, and greed, the Buddhist can live free of hate, sorrow, and greed.

Questions (to be answered in writing)

1. What does science teach about the things in our world which seem hard and solid? 2. Are atoms solid? 3. Are atoms eternal and unchanging? 4. Do atoms have in them a permanent substance? 5. Does science find a soul in man? 6. What do most religions teach about the "soul"? 7. What does Buddhism teach about the existence of the soul? (TO ANSWER QUESTIONS 8-11, LOOK FOR INFORMATION IN AN ENCYCLOPEDIA OR SCHOOL HISTORY BOOK.) 8. What happened at the Witch

trials at Salem, Massachusetts? 9. What is the Massacre of St. Bartholomew's Day? 10. Why was the Inquisition important in Europe? 11. Who was Giordano Bruno and what happened to him?

SUFFERING

"Suffering and the cure of suffering: this only do I teach," said the Buddha.

The Buddha looked squarely at life. He examined its causes, and he thought about its fruits. He examined life the way a scientist does. And, like a scientist, the Buddha made a scientific description of life.

Life, the Buddha Sakyamuni found, is filled with suffering and sorrow. Life is full of friction, anxiety, annoyance and fear. Life is full of irritation, discontent, care, worry, pain, sorrow, and misery.

Birth is suffering. Old age is suffering. Disease is suffering. Death is suffering. It is suffering to be with things and people we do not like. It is painful to be separated from what we love. It is misery to want what we cannot get.

All suffering, anxiety, and worry can be found in one common cause—selfish desire. Man is ruled by a great desire for self-satisfaction. However, this desire for self-satisfaction can never really be fulfilled. This unsatisfied desire, indeed, only produces more suffering and unhappiness.

The origin of all suffering is the desire for pleasure for one's self. This desire finds momentary delight here and there, but it is constantly seeking more permanent and lasting satisfaction.

Suffering is caused by the desire to satisfy the self through the senses. It has its source in clinging to life for the sake of life.

All suffering, anxiety, and unhappiness in all life arise, therefore, from the desire for selfhood. They arise from selfishness, and sorrow is at an end when selfishness is ended.

Anxiety and unhappiness cease when there is no longer any desire for self-satisfaction.

If a person rids himself of selfishness, feelings of disappointment and unhappiness become impossible to him. If a person rids himself of the false idea of self, his life will have in it no anxiety, annoyance, irritation, or worry.

Such a person will be completely indifferent to his own suffering due to poverty, sickness or death. He lives for others, not for himself.

Questions (to be written out)
1. What did the Buddha Sakyamuni say he taught? 2. In what way did the Buddha look at life? 3. What kind of a description of life did Sakyamuni make? 4. With what is life filled? 5. In what common cause do all sorrows and suffering originate? 6. What great desire rules man? 7. What is produced by unsatisfied desire? 8. By what is suffering produced? 9. When does suffering cease? 10. To what is a person indifferent if he had rid himself of the desire for selfhood? 11. For whom does such a person live? 12. How does the idea of an eternal soul lead to suffering?

GRATITUDE
"Let us live happily then," begins a chapter in a famous Buddhist scripture. A happy life is one of the goals of Buddhists.

"Suffering," said Sakyamuni, "and the cure of suffering: this only do I teach." When suffering, anxiety, and fear have been ended, only happiness remains.

Suffering is caused by our selfish desires. The cure of suffering, therefore, is to root out our selfishness. Unselfishness is the key to happiness. The completely unselfish person would live for others, not for himself.

Such complete unselfishness arises from a religious awakening to our interrelationship with everything in the universe.

We live by eating food gathered from every corner of the earth. We listen in our homes to radio programs broadcast from New York or Paris. We watch television from the moon. Our clothes may be made from Australian wool or from silk from China or Japan.

We are thus endlessly interrelated with all and everything in the universe. When we really understand our relation to the whole universe, it makes us very humble. We realize that all our good fortune is due to the efforts of countless others.

When we realize this, our gratitude extends to everything in the universe. It is only with their help that we have ever been able to hear and realize the truth of Buddha's teachings.

To express our gratitude, we then strive to make all beings happy. Our every thought is of all the beings in the universe. We take no thought of ourselves.

The first instant of this perfect selflessness is called by Shinran of the Honganji the "Awakening of Faith." In the instant of this awakening we realize that all things are changing, that all things are soulless, and that all things are suffering. In this instant we lose our selfishness. In this instant we are completely and perfectly unselfish.

Faith, then, according to the Honganji doctrine of Buddhism is an attitude of unselfishness. It causes us to realize our interdependence on every thing in the universe. Through the awakening of such faith, gratitude becomes the motivation of our life.

We are grateful and thankful to all those who made it possible for us to hear the Buddha's teachings. We are grateful to the Buddha for showing us the path to end suffering. We are grateful to the whole universe, and this gratitude is part of our great happiness.

Questions (to be answered in writing)

1. What is one of the chief goals of Buddhism? 2. What did the Buddha teach? 3. What remains when suffering is gotten rid

of? 4. What causes our suffering? 5. What is the cure of suffering? 6. What is the meaning of interrelated? 7. What makes us humble? 8. To whose efforts do we owe our good fortune? 9. How can we express our gratitude? 10. What is "the awakening of faith"? 11. In what instant are we perfectly unselfish? 12. In Shin Buddhism, what is faith? 13. With the awakening of faith, what becomes the motivation of our life?

THE FOUR NOBLE TRUTHS

"Sakya," wrote Shinran of the Honganji, "was born and arose in the world to explain clearly the teaching of the way. He wished to save the masses and extend to them the true reward."

In the Sutra of the Teachings Left by the Buddha, we find Gautama Buddha, the Sage of the Sakya nation, saying, "I am like a good doctor who recognizes the illness and prescribes a medicine: but whether it will actually be taken or not is not up to the doctor."

Sakyamuni Buddha often talked about life in terms that a doctor might use, and it seems he had learned something of medicine among the arts he studied as a young man.

Buddha often preached of "salvation" as though it were the curing of an illness. Sakya's briefest explanation of his teaching, in fact, is merely a statement of the ancient Indian medical method. An Indian doctor was first to discover the disease. Next he had to learn its cause and then seek a way to remove this cause. Finally he must set about to apply this way of removal to the illness. These four steps in the curing of illness became the Four Noble Truths of Buddha's way of salvation.

This Sage of the Sakya nation found life troubled by the illness of Suffering (Dukkha). All living beings suffer; their lives are never completely free of anxiety, fear, pain, sorrow, bane, suffering. The very nature of living creates tension and anxiety.

Suffering is the illness of life. Looking for its cause, the

Great Physician found it in Greed, Hatred, and Ignorance. These three states of mind, the Buddha explained, are the cause of all the anxieties of life.

The Buddha Sakyamuni then realized there is a way of removing these anxieties. It is simply to remove their cause as a doctor does a cancer. It is to cut out of one's life all Greed, Hatred and Ignorance.

The curing of life's Suffering is found in the medicine of the Buddha prescribed. This cure is the Noble Eightfold Path. This is a way of life which lessens our sufferings in life, even though we live it imperfectly as ordinary men. For the ordinary man, indeed, the Noble Eightfold Path is the highest guide for living in this world.

"The moon might grow hot, and the sun might grow cold, but the four truths which Buddha taught cannot change," says the Sutra of the Teachings Left by the Buddha. "The truth of suffering which Buddha taught, is of real suffering which cannot become joy. Accumulation of desires truly is its cause, and there can never be a different cause. If suffering is destroyed, it is when its cause has been destroyed. If the cause is destroyed, its result is destroyed. The way of destroying error is the path of truth, and there is no other path."

Questions (to be answered in writing)

1. Why was Sakya Buddha born? 2. What did the Buddha say he was? 3. Does the Buddha force people to be saved? 4. What are the four parts of ancient Indian medical method? 5. What is the meaning of "Sage"? 6. What is the meaning of "anxiety"? 7. What does "bane" mean? 8. What is the illness of life? 9. What three things are the cause of suffering? 10. What 'medicine' did the Buddha prescribe to cure the illness of life? 11. What are the Four Noble Truths?

THE FIRST NOBLE TRUTH

"There are four boons," says a Buddhist scripture, "which no priest nor sage, no god or devil, no highest being, can obtain. What are these four? That old age and decay should never set in; that illness and pain should never trouble one; that death should never snatch one away; that the fruit of bad deeds should never ripen. Truly these four boons can never be obtained, even by a priest or sage, or by a god or devil, or even by any highest being, nor by anyone in all the world."

These four boons include all the things which would give mankind peace of mind. Yet, nowhere can we find these four boons being enjoyed by man.

Everywhere man finds his life brief and transient. We wish to live forever, but we grow old and die. We want health and happiness, but we find illness and unhappiness. Life is an uneven process. Our joys are nearly balanced by our worries.

Frustration, fear, and failure are seldom far from satisfaction, courage, and success. We have no lasting peace of mind, we seem unable to enjoy permanent happiness.

This lack of peace of mind is the unhealthly condition which the Buddha, the Great Physician of the world, seeks to cure by his teachings.

All existence is connected with suffering, frustration, anxiety, fear, pain, sorrow. These are found in the lives of every sentient being. This lack of peace of mind brings us to a constant recurrence of anxiety.

This situation the Buddha likened to all illness from which the world is suffering. Like all illnesses it can be cured with the help of a good physician and proper medicines.

The cure of the ills of existence brings us peace of mind. The cure starts when we recognize the illness for what it is. This is the First Noble Truth, that all existence is involved in suffering and sorrow.

Questions (to be answered in writing)

1. What is the meaning of "boon"? 2. What does "Sage" mean? 3. What does "transient" mean? 4. Does anyone have the four boons? 5. What does mankind want in life? 6. What does the Buddha seek to cure? 7. What does the cure of suffering bring mankind? 8. What is the First Noble Truth?

THE SECOND NOBLE TRUTH

That mankind finds no peace of mind in every-day living can be seen everywhere. What is the cause of this uneasiness which is deep-rooted in man's subconsciousness? This is the first great question a physician must answer before he can cure the illness.

Sakyamuni, the Physician of the World, saw the illness of mankind, and he looked for its cause. From the symptoms, he could see that the cause of man's unhappiness was greed, hate, and delusion.

Mankind is under the delusion of his own self-importance. We think the universe revolves around man; and we try, when we find Nature otherwise, to change the whole of the universe.

As individuals, we like to think our own little world revolves around us. We all, at times, act overbearing and pompous. We forget and ignore the rights and wishes of others.

When, as it often happens, other people remind us of their wishes, we come to hate them. We hate people and things because they stand in our way. We hate everthing and everyone that stops us from getting what we want.

Mankind is, after all, filled with greed for money, or power, or whatever he thinks will give him happiness. The greed is a driving power deep in our subconsciousness. We want what we want, and we mean to have it.

Thus we see that our lack of peace of mind has its cause in greed and hate which are closely connected with our delusions of

15

self-importance. Greed, hate, and delusion cannot really be separated. Greed is delusion in practice; hate is delusion in practice. Delusion is that state of mind when hate and greed blind us to truth.

These three—greed, hate, and delusion—are the cause of all the sorrow and suffering of mankind. These three, which are only different aspects of absolute desire, are the cause of all the ills of existence.

This is the Second Noble Truth, that the cause of all the suffering and sorrow of existence is desire.

Questions (to be answered in writing)
1. What is the first great question a physician must ask? 2. What is the cause of man's unhappiness? 3. What is the meaning of "delusion"? 4. What is the chief delusion of mankind? 5. What does "overbearing" mean? 6. What is the meaning of "pompous"? 7. Why do we hate people? 8. What is the meaning of "subconsciousness"? 9. What does "desire" mean? 10. What is the Second Noble Truth?

THE THIRD NOBLE TRUTH

The idea of ending suffering is the very center of Buddhism. "Suffering and the cure of suffering: this only do I teach," said the Buddha. The ending or annihilation of suffering is the goal of Buddhism.

Some people say Buddhism is sorrowful. They say the Buddha's teachings are pessimistic. They think this way because Buddha talks of suffering. Suffering, anxiety, frustration are sad states of mind. A religion that talks only of sadness would be pessimistic. But Buddhism does not talk only of suffering.

The Buddha did not need to tell the world about suffering. People see it. They feel it. They fear and dread it. Everyone learns about suffering. They learn when their dear ones die. They learn when duty separates them from those they love. They learn when they cannot have the things they want. The Buddha's teachings would be meaningless if they only told mankind that there is suffering in the world.

The importance of the Buddha's teachings lie in the cure of suffering. This is a teaching of the end of suffering. It is a teaching that leads to the annihilation of suffering. Thus, Buddhism is a religion of joy and happiness. Buddhism is not pessimistic; it is optimistic.

Buddhism is an optimistic religion because it teaches that there is an end to suffering. It teaches that suffering can be annihilated. It teaches that joy, happiness, and peace are possible.

Buddhism is an optimistic religion because it teaches that greed, hate, delusion can be ended. It teaches that ignorance can be ended. These things which cause our suffering can be annihilated from our lives.

The Third Noble Truth, the annihilation of suffering, makes Buddhism a religion of hope. The ending of suffering brings joy and serenity. The annihilation of suffering is the very center of Buddhism.

Questions (to be answered in writing)

1. What does "annihilation" mean? 2. What is the goal of Buddhism? 3. What does "pessimistic" mean? 4. Why do some people say Buddhism is pessimistic? 5. Did people know, before Buddha taught, that there was suffering in the world? 6. What is important in the Buddha's teachings? 7. What does "optimistic" mean? 8. Why is Buddha's teaching optimistic? 9. Why is Buddhism a religion of hope?

THE FOURTH NOBLE TRUTH

The remedy for suffering is the Noble Eightfold Path. This is the path of truth. It can be trod at two levels. Those who have not attained spiritual awareness walk the path in a worldly way. Those who have attained to spiritual awareness walk the path at a higher level.

The first step of the Noble Eightfold Path is Right Views. Right Views is to see life as it really is. Right Views is to see that all things are suffering. It is to see that all things are impermanent. It is to see that all things are without a permanent soul or ego. It is to understand that sorrow can be ended by putting an end to desire.

The second step is Right Mindedness. Right Mindedness is to have friendly thoughts. It is to be without prejudice. It is to treat all forms of life equally.

The third step is Right Speech. This means to speak kindly and truthfully. Right Speech is to tell the truth in all things.

The fourth step is Right Action. This is to act skillfully and kindly. It means to go through life sympathetically. Right Action is to live without vanity or violence.

The fifth step is Right Livelihood. This is to earn one's living without hurting others. It means to work at a lawful job. It means to work at a job which will not increase your own desires.

The sixth step is Right Endeavor. Right Endeavor is trying to avoid evil. It is rejecting bad and lowly things. It is trying to foster noble qualities.

The seventh step is Right Mindfulness. This is to have the Buddha's truth always in mind. It means to reflect this truthful mindfulness in love, compassion, joy and equal mindedness. It means to have one's mind filled with the love and wisdom of Buddhahood.

The last step of the Noble Eightfold Path is Right Concentration. Right Concentration is organizing the mind. It is directing the mind. It is bringing the mind to singlepointedness. The mind becomes as sharp as a sword. It sees the highest truth clearly, sharply.

Questions (to be answered in writing)

1. How many ways are there to tread the Noble Eightfold Path? 2. What is the first step of the Eightfold Path? 3. What is meant by Right Views? 4. What is the second Step of the Path? 5. What kind of thought does one have at the second step? 6. What is the third step of the Path? 7. What kind of speech is taught at the third step? 8. What is the fourth step? 9. What kinds of acts should one do in passing through life? 10. What is the fifth step? 11. How should one earn his living? 12. What is the sixth step? 13. In life, what should one try to do? 14. What is the seventh step of the Path? 15. What should always be in one's mind? 16. What kinds of thoughts should one have? 17. What is the eighth step? 18. What does the word "concentration" mean? 19. What happens in Right Concentration?

KARMA

From ancient times, one verse of the scriptures has been thought to be the very heart of Buddhism. When pious people wanted to erect a stupa but had no relic of Buddha to enshrine there, this verse has been written out and used in the stupa instead of a relic. This single verse, then, is considered the very equal of a Buddha! It says: "The Awakened One has made known how all things come from Cause; the Great Saint has also told how they pass away again." This truth is the heart of Buddhism. This principle or law of cause and effect is called Conditioned Origination.

Many people confuse this teaching of Conditioned Origination with another Buddhist teaching known as karma. Karma has, indeed, become an English word. It is found in many dictionaries. It is used, moreover, by many who are not Buddhist. Such people usually understand karma to be fate, destiny, predestination. They say that karma is the inevitable result of a person's good or bad deeds. But Buddhists do not understand karma in this way.

For Buddhists, karma is not the law of cause and effect. It is not the same as fate, inevitable destiny, or predestination.

Karma literally means action. It comes from the same word-root as the English word create. Karma is willed action. That is, karma is an action which in our hearts we want to do. It is an action based upon our wants, our desires. The Buddha said: "Having willed, one acts by body, speech and thought." Karma, then, is a willed action of the body, mouth, or mind. The action (karma) may be talked about in past time or in the present. A karmic action, a willed action, arises from the will expressed as desire. Every karmic action is rooted in the desires of the will; these desires of the will are, simply put, complete selfishness.

In existence, every karmic action produces a result or effect. Part of every action is the power of producing an effect, just as a seed has the power to produce a flower. The doing of a deed is transient; it is the action of an instant. Its form, however, is permanent. The sight of an object, the thinking of a thought, the doing of an act, all these pass away; but they leave traces which endure and evolve. What a man does in the world is important, but, for Buddhism, what a man does in his mind is even more important. Willful actions leave traces in the mind. These traces are called conformations (sankharas).

The conformations or sankharas are the mind's dispositions, memory structures. These conformations make a man's character and his personality. Karma-actions we likened to a seed; the conformations, then, are the soil, and the personality is the flower. When the flower blooms, the seed no longer exists. It is, then, not correct to use the word karma for the flower or result of an action.

The effect of a karma-action is not fated, predestined, or automatic. What we have done in the past has made us what we are today. What we are now, this very instant, doing is making our future. We ourselves create our own future; it is not fated or predestined. This, indeed, is the very foundation of the religious life as the Buddha taught: "If anyone says that a man must reap according to his deeds, in that case there is no religious life nor any possibility for the entire extinction of misery. But if one says that the reward a man reaps accords with his deeds, in that case there is a religious life, and there is the opportunity for religious life." (Anguttara-nikaya, iii. 99). If man must reap according to his deeds, he is bound by fate; he cannot escape his destiny. But when one reaps in accordance with his deeds, it is possible to escape from sorrow and suffering.

A seed, once planted and watered, begins to grow. But the water can be withheld or the flower can be cut off when it is still in bud, so it never flowers. So it is with the teaching of karma which gives consolation, hope, strength and moral courage to the faithful Buddhist. When something unexpected arises in his life, when he meets difficulties, misfortunes, unhappiness, he knows that he is reaping in accordance with what he has sown in his own actions. Instead of giving up, leaving everything to fate, he makes a strenuous effort to pull up the weeds or cut them off before they blossom and create more seed; he tries to sow useful seed in place of the weeds. The future is entirely in his own hands, and he can become the kind of person he wants to be. Desire, will, is the cause of karmas and karmic action is the cause of the cycle of rebirth. Therefore, Buddhists insist, it is possible at any time to break the chain of rebirth. One has only to get rid of desire, and causation stops.

This view is not held, of course, by all people who make use of the word karma. Hindus and even some Christian also use the word karma. To many, karma is a burden or debt of sin which is, so to speak, stored in a "bank" and must be paid off, item by item. This means that the individual is bound almost indefinitely to the cycle of birth and death, while he vainly tries to do one good deed for each bad deed he has done. Others, as we have said, wrongly equate karma with the chain of Conditioned Origination. But karma is only one link in the chain of Conditioned Origination.

This doctrine of conditioned origination is the very core of

Buddha's teaching. By applying this to personality, we see how character arises by Conditioned Origination. From (1) Ignorance, rooted in desire, hatred and delusion, arise (2) Actions (karma). From Actions arise (3) Consciousness. Consciousness determines (4) Name-and-form, and Name-and-form give rise to (5) Sense. By Sense, (6) Contact is determined; by Contact arises (7) Feeling. Feeling determines (8) Craving, and Craving in its turn gives rise to (9) Grasping. From Grasping arises (10) Becoming; Becoming determines (11) Birth. By Birth is determined (12) Age-and-Death, Sorrow and Grief, Woe, Lamentation, and Despair. Such is the arising of all the suffering, anxiety, frustration, and sorrow which are the human character.

When the Buddhist understands thus that he is himself his own creator, he sees karma and conditioned origination as the reason for his efforts to live bravely. This insight kindles his enthusiasm and sharpens his sense of individual responsibility for actions. It gives rise to a universal love which is shown in his doing good purely for the sake of his fellow sentient beings. He becomes kind, considerate, tolerant, generous.

Questions (to be answered in writing)

1. What verse has been regarded as the equal of the Buddha? 2. What is the name of the law of cause and effect in Buddhism? 3. Is Karma the same as the law of conditioned origination? 4. What is the literal meaning of the word karma? 5. What is karma? 6. What are "conformations"? 7. Who creates our future? 8. Does man reap his fate according to his karma? 9. What is the cause of karma? 10. What are the twelve elements of the chain of Conditioned Origination? 11. If a Buddhist speaks of a "creator" to what does he refer?

LIBERATION

To Buddhist, the goal of this life is liberation.   Liberation means release from all the fetters which bind men to this life. There are ten chief fetters or bonds. Bound by these fetters, mankind goes on suffering in life. These ten fetters are merely another way of dividing and studying desire.

1. Attachment to the notion of an eternal self
2. Doubt
3. Attachment to ceremonies and ritual
4. Sensuality
5. Ill-will
6. Desire for earthly life
7. Desire for future life
8. Conceit
9. Self-righteousness
10. Ignorance

Liberation is being saved from these fetters. Most other religions talk about salvation. But Buddhists talk about liberation, or sometimes release.

Liberation is the goal of this life. We seek liberation here and now. This is an important happening in our lives. There are many stages to liberation. Not all people give up all fetters at once.

The first stage of liberation is to give up the first three fetters. This first stage has many names. Shinran calls it the Awakening of Faith and Peace of Mind. It is also called the Bodhicitta (the thought of Enlightenment).

The person who is liberated is called a Stream-enterer. His liberation has put him in the stream which will flow to Complete Nirvana. He is also called a Bodhisattva, because he is a seeker (sattva) after Enlightenment (bodhi).

Stream-entry is the first important religious step. It is the first real step toward Nirvana's peace. This freedom from the three fetters makes certain the final attainment of Complete Nirvana. Freeing yourself from these fetters is like planting a seed which will grow into Nirvana.

Questions (to be answered in writing)

1. What is the dictionary meaning of "Liberation"? 2. What is a "fetter"? 3. What are the first three fetters? 4. What word do most other religions use in place of liberation? 5. When should we find liberation? 6. Is liberation a one-stage experience? 7. What does Shinran call liberation? 8. What does bodhicitta mean? 9. What is a Stream-enterer? 10. What is the first important religious step in Buddhism?

FAITH

Shin Buddhism speaks a great deal about faith. There are some people who say this makes it just like Christianity. Some people also say faith has no place in original Buddhism; but this is not the fact.

The Buddha said: "Faith is the wealth here (in this world) best for men." (Sutta-nipata). In the same scripture he said: "By faith, did Vakkalin, Alivi-Gotama and Bhadravudha win release (into Nirvana)." (verse 1146). Faith, then, is part of original Buddhism, and faith does give Nirvana.

Of course, there are several meanings to the word faith in Buddhist usage. At one level, faith means merely simple confidence. A man may have confidence that there is something of value in Buddhist teachings. This simple faith prompts him to look deeper into these doctrines. Still, he may not believe them to be true. A deeper faith prompts a man to practice Buddha's teachings in his own life; this is a trust in the ultimate truth of Buddhism. This faith is a belief based on the best possible evidence of the truth of Buddhism. Such evidence is in the logical reasonableness of the teachings and in the living example of the Buddha and that long line of saints who have attained Nirvana to this very day. The Buddha himself told us to accept nothing even on his word alone, but to test all things and know for ourselves the truth of Buddhism.

An entirely different kind of faith, however, is that faith which brings us to Nirvana. This faith, which Shinran calls the awakening of faith, peace of mind, single-pointedness of mind, is a single instant of perfect egolessness. It is a single instant when we are free from all selfishness. In that instant, absolute truth fills our heart. Shinran teaches us that this instant is free from all double-mindedness (that is, free from all doubt). At this instant we crush the three fetters of doubt, attachment to self, and attachment to rite and ritual. Because this instant is a moment of perfect egolessness, we do not know when it is upon us: we cannot say, "I am egoless," for the very I which says this would be the ego!

After we have had this awakening of faith, of course, we may think that we had it at some period in the past; but we can never say for certain that we had this at some particular time or place. Indeed, one of the effects of this awakening is a loss of concern with the question of whether or not we had had it.

Shin faith, then, means a single instant of perfect egolessness which has continuing effects in our lives. But is this the same as Christian faith?

Faith is one of the cornerstones of Christianity. The Apostle Paul, in a letter to the Corinthians, listed faith along with hope and charity as the three essentials of the Christian religion. St. Thomas Aquinas taught that it was a great sin not to have faith. He said that infidels (those without faith) should be forced to believe. He taught also that persons who lost their faith should not be tolerated; and Thomas Aquinas went on to say that backsliders who rejoin the faithful and then fall again into unbelief should be allowed to repent, but still they should be killed (Summa Theologia 2-2,1-16). Faith, then, for the Christian is highly important.

It is however, not easy to say what Christian faith is. The most famous Christian definition of faith is in Paul's letter to the

Hebrews: "Faith is the substance of things hoped for, the evidence of things not seen." This does not make much sense. Everyone talks about it, but no one has clearly said what this sentence really means.

Augustine, an early Christian saint, asked, "What is faith but believing what you do not see?" (Joannis Evang Tract c40:8). Actually, however, Christians never seem to use faith in the sense of believing what you do not see. Christians do not see the thunder any more than we do; yet, in the Christian sense, one cannot say: "I have faith it is thundering." The word faith, in the Christian sense, cannot be used loosely.

According to the New Schaff-Herzog Religious Encyclopedia, "Faith, in the New Testament sense, is man's perception of the spiritual and moral order of experience and life offered to man by God in Christ. But it is more than a perception. It is the supreme form of will-power in man. By faith he perceives, and in faith he wills and, under God, ordains the moral equality and the moral end of human history."

Faith, then, for the Christian is the willful determination to believe. But for the Shin Buddhist, faith is a moment of perfect egolessness. Thus, it is free of the will, for the will is the product of the ego. Shin faith is freedom from the ego. It is liberation from the base fetters. It is a form of release. Thus, the word faith means something quite different in Shin Buddhism from what it means in Christianity.

Questions (to be answered in writing)

1. What wealth did the Buddha say was best for men? 2. What does faith mean at a very elementary level? 3. What is the result of a deeper faith? 4. Does Buddhism teach men to accept doctrines just because the Buddha taught them? 5. What are two other names for the Awakening of Faith? 6. Can we know the exact instant we have the first awakening of faith? 7. What does faith mean in Shin Buddhism? 8. Is Saint Thomas Aquinas toler-

ant of people who lose their faith in Christianity? 9. Of what is Christian faith the "supreme form"? 10. What produces the "will"? 11. How does Shin and Christian ideas of "faith" differ?

THE PRECEPTS

Unlike the founders of some religions, the Buddha did not set down any commandments, which all his followers must obey or go to hell. But he did advise many things. These things that he advised are called precepts. There are some precepts for the monks alone. There are other precepts for the nuns alone. Some precepts are for both monks and nuns. Other precepts are for the lay followers. A few precepts are for everyone.

Following the precepts helps to develop good states of mind. Ignoring the precepts makes the mind sink to lower states. There are five precepts which all people are urged to follow. These are called the Panca-Sila. Panca means "Five" and sila means "Custom" or "Habit". These five precepts lead to a human state of mind.

The five precepts which the Buddha taught are:
1. Not to kill
2. Not to lie
3. Not to be unchaste
4. Not to steal
5. Not to lose your senses through alcoholic drinks or drugs.

These five precepts are not just advice to Buddhists. They are precepts or teachings for all mankind. These five precepts are advice for all men.

People who do not observe these five customs are not quite human. They are little better than animals. Animals, indeed, often cannot help acting the way they do. They act by instinct. But men have brains and hearts. They have minds which they can use. If they do not use their minds to show them what is right, how do they differ from animals?

People who do not try to live by right customs find many excuses for themselves. They often say, "I can do anything I want as long as I hurt nobody but myself. If I smoke, or if I get drunk, nobody is hurt but me!" They say such things about each of the five silas.

To kill hurts the person killed, of course. And the killer suffers in prison. But all society is hurt as well. The parents of the dead person, and the parents of the killer are crushed with sorrow. Often wives and children suffer for the rest of their lives because of a killing. And this is true not of mankind alone. When a mother animal is killed, its young often dies from lack of care. Many animals have been killed off by mankind. When this happens, the balance of nature is upset. Then all men suffer.

Many people are hurt by lying, too. The liar may lose his good name, but other people, also, will be hurt. Unchastity and stealing also hurt more people than the one who does the action.

With smoking, drugs, and over use of alcohol this is true: many people beside the user are hurt. Smoking leads to cancer, heart trouble, and many diseases which can kill the user before his time. When he dies or is crippled for life, his friends and relatives must help him. They must take care of his wife and children. They must take care of the person until he dies.

When people do not observe the five precepts, they injure all other men. When people do not observe the five precepts they are hurting themselves too. They destroy good and happy states of mind, and slowly they become satisfied with unhealthy states of mind.

People ignore these precepts through selfishness. They do not care about the feelings of others. They think only of themselves. They think that other people do not matter.

Selfish people break the precepts. But all society is based upon the observance of the precepts. These five precepts are the basis of all morality. If one person is to have his rights respected, all people must observe the precepts. They are the universal customs which allow society to exist. When these five precepts are ignored, all men are attacked and hurt.

Questions (to be answered in writing)

1. What does "commandment" mean? 2. What does "precept" mean? 3. How many precepts did the Buddha give for all mankind? 4. What is another name for the Five Precepts or customs? 5. What is the first Precept? 6. What is the second Precept? 7. What is the third Precept? 8. What is the fourth Precept? 9. What is the fifth Precept? 10. To what do the observance of the Five Precepts lead? 11. What does the word "observe" mean? 12. How is one selfish who breaks the first Precept? 13. How is one selfish who breaks the second Precept? 14. How is one selfish who breaks the third Precept? 15. How is one selfish who breaks the fourth Precept? 16. How is one selfish who breaks the fifth Precept?

THE TEN GOODNESSES

Right thinking Buddhists try to cultivate the ten Goodnesses. Some people cultivate these to bring themselves to religious awareness. Others cultivate the ten Goodnesses out of gratitude. Selfish, conceited, and greedy people cannot practice these ten Goodnesses.

The ten Goodnesses are: non-killing, non-stealing, chastity, non-lying, not being double-tongued, non-use of coarse language, non-use of filthy language, not being covetous, not being angry, and not holding to perverted views. The opposite of these are the Ten Evils.

Non-killing is more than refusing to take life. It means to help sentient beings to live full and useful lives. It means to help people to get enough food for healthy lives. It means to help people get the proper medicine and medical treatment. It means to promote the hopes and ideals of people. It means to help sentient beings to fulfill their highest potentialities.

Non-stealing means more than rejecting thievery. Non-stealing means not to deprive others of their rights. To litter the highways, for example, robs others of a beautiful sight; they lose the experience of a clean and lovely highway. We steal other's happiness when we treat them as less than equal. We steal other's rights whenever we do anything to deprive them of the freedom to be themselves.

Being chaste means more than abstaining from improper sex relations. It means to keep ourselves pure and free of using other people to satisfy our selfish desires. Every impure thought is unchaste. Whenever we use people as though they were things, we are unchaste.

Not lying is more than just telling the truth. Sometimes even telling the truth is misleading. Sometimes speaking the truth hurts a person's feelings. "You are a fat slob!" Such statements may be the truth, but they are still a kind of lie. It is the truth because the person is fat. But it is a lie, because the speaker really wants to say or do something else. Perhaps he wants to hurt the other person physically; but he doesn't dare. The statement is factual truth, but it is not made out of a sincere and kind heart. Real non-lying is what is spoken from a kind and generous heart.

To be double-tongued is more than speaking untruth. It is to speak so that every sentence has two meanings. The double-tongued or fork-tongued person speaks so that he means one thing, but he hopes his listener will understand his words in a different way. Thus, the double-tongued person hopes to achieve his own selfish ends. He wants others to misunderstand him, because this will work to his advantage.

Coarse language is rough and rude speech. It shows a selfish attitude in the speaker. It means the speaker is trying to ignore the rights of the listener. The speaker wants only to dominate others. Therefore, coarse language is fundamentally evil. The good Buddhist tries never to use it.

Buddhists also try not to use filthy or foul language. Filthy language offends many people. Only selfish and mean people offend others. Thus Buddhists try not to use foul language. But filthy language also plants the seeds of filth in one's own innermost mind. So the use of filthy language can make one's own mind become foul and filthy.

Not to become angry is more than just controlling one's temper. It means to actually love the object of your annoyance. Not to become angry means to speak softly and pleasantly when others speak badly. It means to love those who hate you; it means to love those who are angry with you. Anger is a sign of selfish conceit. Not to be angry means to cultivate humility and love. It means to cultivate understanding and concern.

Not to be covetous is to be free of jealousy. It is to be free of desire for others' possessions. But not to be covetous means also to be free with one's own belongings. It means to be generous. To give to those in need all that they need.

Not to hold perverted views means to seek after the truth. It means to free oneself from unreasonable ideas and notions. It means to be logical; it means to use one's reason. It means not to hold to one's own conceited views, insisting all follow them. Not to hold perverted views means to respect the opinions of others. It means to listen to their ideas, but not to accept them unless they are reasonable and accord with the truth. But not to hold perverted views does not mean we should deny others their rights. We must allow others to follow their own views, even when we know those views are wrong.

These, then, are the ten Goodnesses. Buddhists cultivate them for the benefit they bring. These Goodnesses benefit oneself and they benefit others. They help to make the universe a better place to live in. Sentient beings are made happy and unselfish by their cultivation.

Questions (to be answered in writing)
1. What are two reasons people practice the Ten Goodnesses? 2. What is the meaning of the first Goodness? 3. What is the meaning of the second Goodness? 4. What is the meaning of the third Goodness? 5. What is the meaning of the fourth Goodness?

6. What is the meaning of the fifth Goodness? 7. What is the meaning of the sixth Goodness? 8. What is the meaning of the seventh Goodness? 9. What is the meaning of the eighth Goodness? 10. What is the meaning of the ninth Goodness? 11. What is the meaning of the tenth Goodness? 12. Who is benefited by the cultivation of the Ten Goodnesses?

TOWARDS BUDDHAHOOD

Ordinary man is filled with greed, hate and delusion. He is ruled by his desires. He is led about by his passions. He is tossed through life as a leaf is tossed in the wind. But he does not see his own condition. He does not know that he is ignorant and blind.

One day, however, something happens to each ordinary man. It may be that he meets a saint. It may be that he hears a sermon. Or, perhaps, he reads a scripture. Whatever it is, the ordinary man opens his eyes. He sees, for the first time, that he lacks something. He knows that he is suffering. He knows that he is filled with anxiety. He knows that he is ignorant of the cause of his suffering. The ordinary man now starts searching. He seeks a way of overcoming his suffering, anxiety, and frustration. He may seek through many lives, for he does not, at first, seek with all his devotion. He knows he lacks peace of mind. But his occasional joys and happinesses help him to forget his true condition.

At his earliest stage, then the ordinary man is entirely led by his passions; but he does not know his condition. Then he hears of the Truth. He begins to understand that he lacks Truth and Peace in his heart. From time to time he seeks the Truth.

As he searches, he comes finally to religious experience. Looking back upon his past, we may say that this was a gradual process. It may have been eons since first he became dimly aware that he was ruled by his passions. But his religious experience was, in itself, a matter of an instant. Therefore, we sometimes say that this experience is sudden.

The religious experience, which is critical in man's existence, is called Liberation. It is also called Release, the Awakening of Faith, Satori, Peace of Mind, and many other names.   In this first really religious awakening we are largely freed from the first three fetters. These fetters bind man to the round of rebirth.

An ordinary man who reaches this level of Liberation is called a Stream-enterer. He has, at last, entered this stream leading to Nirvana. This religious experience, accordingly, is crucial. Until an ordinary man enters the stream, his attainment of Nirvana is not fixed and determined. When a man has entered the stream, he is sure and certain to attain Nirvana. He has, of course, not attained Nirvana. He is not completely Enlightened. But it is now certain that sometime in the future he will reach Nirvana and Enlightenment.

The Stream-enterer will grow spiritually, when he abandons two further fetters, he becomes a Once-returner. This means that in his very next life he will attain Nirvana. Or, if he abandons the first five fetters completely and perfectly, he becomes a Non-returner. When man abandons all ten fetters he becomes an Arahat.

An Arahat attains to the same complete Enlightenment as a Buddha. The Arahat differs from the Buddha in one way only. The Arahat attains Enlightenment and Nirvana in this world. However, he has followed the path laid down by the Buddha. The Arahat can hear the Buddha's teachings in person or through the scriptures. He has heard the Buddha's message in sermons and lectures. Therefore, the Arahat has followed the Buddha to Enlightenment.

A Buddha, on the other hand, discovers the truth for himself. Through eons of seeking, the Buddha seeks Enlightenment. He finally arises in a world where the Dharma is not known. Then he discovers the teachings of the Dharma in his own mind. He cuts all the fetters. He destroys his own ignorance, greed, hatred and delusion. In the religious experience of Enlightenment, the Buddha becomes completely filled with wisdom and mercy. But he does this without the advantage of sutras, sermons, and teachers. Moreover, the Buddha teaches his discovery to all mankind. He seeks to bring all sentient beings to perfect freedom and love. In this he differs from the Arahat, who usually lives quietly in retirement.

Ordinary man, then, when he attains to release, can go on to become an Arahat. He may first pass through the stages of the Stream-enterer, Once-returner, and then Arahat. He may also pass from the stage of the Stream-enterer to that of the Non-returner. He can pass directly from one stage to the next. Indeed, some people, in their first religious experience, pass directly to the stage of the Non-returner. A Non-returner, of course, does not go on to the stage of the normal Arahat. The Non-returner may become Buddha at the instant of his death; he may attain Buddhahood after he has died, but without being born in another life.

One path to Enlightenment, then, is marked by the stages of the Stream-enterer, the Once-returner, and the Arahat. But there is a second method. It, too, leads to Enlightenment. And many people who begin the first path change to the second. The Buddha Sakyamuni did. Most often this change is made just before a person becomes an Arahat, but it can be made earlier.

At one point in his religious growth, a person may decide that he does not want Nirvana for himself alone. He sees sentient beings suffering. He wants to help free them. The universes are filled with suffering, frustrated beings. The seeker feels deep compassion for them. He wants to bring them peace and happiness. Therefore, he decided that he must himself become a Buddha and teach all sentient beings. The seeker feels that for him to accept arahatship would be selfish. At this point he develops the Bodhi-attitude. Bodhi means enlightenment. The seeker develops an attitude or idea that he must himself save all sentient beings. He therefore turns from the goal of arahatship. To become an Arahat would restrict him; he could not bring all sentient beings to Nirvana. This attitude leads the seeker to become a Buddha. He decides that however hard the task, he will discover Enlightenment for himself. He will then teach it in a world which has never heard it. This resolution is called the Bodhi-attitude, the Bodhi-mind, the Bodhi-heart.

After the seeker has attained the Bodhi-attitude, he is called a bodhisattva. A bodhisattva is a seeker after full and complete Enlightenment. He undertakes the practices of the Bodhisattva. These practices are chiefly the paramitas or perfections. There are ten paramitas. They are: dana (donation); sila (rules or morality), patience, energetic action, dhyana (meditation), wisdom, adaptability, vows, purpose, and knowledge. The bodhisattva gives generously of his wealth and possessions. But, most of all, he gives himself. He gives his time, his love, his help to all in need. He practices the customs or rules or morality. He is patient and understanding with all. He is especially patient with people who try to annoy him. He acts energetically to help anyone in need. He practices calmness in his mind. He cultivates wisdom. He practices adapting his teachings and his actions to the people he teaches. To the educated, he preaches the truth in an educated way; to the uneducated person, he preaches by adapting his teaching of the same truth to the understanding of the listener. The bodhisattva vows to save all sentient beings. He strengthens his purpose to fulfill his vows. And the bodhisattva acquires knowledge for the benefit of all sentient beings.

When the bodhisattva has perfected all the paramitas, he becomes a Buddha. He attains to full and Perfect Enlightenment. As a Buddha, he preaches the truth to all who will listen.

Questions (to be answered in writing)

1. With what is the ordinary man filled? 2. How does the ordinary man understand his original condition? 3. What are some ways that may remove the dust from the eyes of the ordinary man? 4. When the dust is removed from the eyes of the ordinary man, what does he begin to understand? 5. Is the development of spirituality a gradual process? 6. In what way may it be said that spiritual experience is sudden? 7. What are five names for the first

great, crucial experience in man's religious growth? 8. What is a Stream-enterer? 9. What is fixed and determined by entering the stream? 10. What fetters does a stream-enterer cut off in part? 11. What fetters are cut partially by the once-returner? 12. How does an ordinary man become a non-returner? 13. How does an Arahat differ from a Buddha? 14. What does a Buddha discover? 15. What decision does a seeker make to become a bodhisattva? 16. What does bodhi mean? 17. What is a bodhisattva? 18. What are the paramitas? 19. What are the ten paramitas? 20. When does a bodhisattva become a Buddha?

BUDDHISM IN INDIA

Seven days after the Buddha died there was a meeting of some monks. Subhadra was at this meeting. He was an old monk. To the other monks, Subhadra said: "We are well rid of Gautama. He was always telling us what to do. This is good; that is bad. He was always ordering us about. Now he is dead, and we can do what we want."

When Kasyapa, the famous elder monk, heard these words, he was unhappy. Kasyapa thought that the Buddha's teaching might soon die out. If everyone did what he wanted, taught what he wanted, then the Buddha-dharma would disappear. Kasyapa thought about the problem. Finally he had an idea. He spoke to the other monks. He said that there should be a big meeting of the best monks. They would all recite what they heard from the Buddha's lips. When the rainy season came, five hundred great monks gathered in a cave. There all the teachings were recited. Different groups among the monks agreed to memorize and hand down different portions of the scriptures.

When the rainy season was over, another monk came to their meeting. The five hundred told him what they had done. This monk said that they had done a good thing. It was good that they preserve the teachings of Buddha. But, he said, he too had heard the teachings from Buddha's own lips. And, he said, he would continue to remember them as he had received them from the Buddha. The five hundred monks did not disagree.

There were probably many other monks like this one. They had heard the Buddha teach. They remembered his teachings, and they handed them down to their disciples. So little groups arose that had slightly different collections of sutras.

Once the Buddha had told Ananda that it would be all right to change the unimportant rules after the Buddha's death. But Ananda did not bother to ask which rules for the monks were important. After the Buddha's death most monks agreed that it was now too late to change the rules. But some rules were not clear. For example, monks were not to use gold-money. Could they then use paper money? There were many kinds of problems. In India's hot plains monks were allowed only three thin garments. Might they wear more in the nothern mountains where there is snow the year around? As problems arose, different groups of monks decided in different ways.

Thus, some groups started about problems of rules. Other groups started because of remembering the scriptures in different ways. These grew into sects. It is said that three hundred years after the Buddha there were eighteen sects of Buddhism.

About two hundred fifty years after the Buddha's death, Asoka became Emperor of India. In cruel wars he conquered most of India and Pakistan. He killed thousands upon thousands of soldiers in war. Then Asoka was converted to Buddhism. He stopped his wars. He tried to rule wisely and justly. He sent Buddhist missionaries to many countries.

At this time many bad people had become Buddhist monks. Asoka had the bad monks kicked out of the monkhood. He wrote the words of Buddha on stone pillars so all could see them.

About two hundred years after Asoka, another great king arose. His name was Kanishka. He, too, believed in Buddhism. He had all the scriptures written on metal plates. He built many monuments to remember the Buddha. He had a great meetng of monks to help make Buddhism strong and pure.

About the time of Kanishka, there was a very famous monk named Asvaghosa. Asvaghosa wrote many beautiful poems and plays. These helped to spread Buddhism all over India. Many of his writings are still read.

By the second century of the Common Era, Indian Buddhism was divided into two forms. One was Mahayana, which means the Great Vehicle. The other was called Hinayana by the Mahayanists. Hinayana means Little Vehicle. The chief difference in the two was the scriptures they read and studied.

The greatest Mahayana scholars were Nagarjuna and Vasubandhu. Nagarjuna lived about 150 of the Common Era. He wrote commentaries on many scriptures, and he also wrote many original essays and poems. He especially taught that all things are empty of any eternal characteristic. Vasubandhu lived about 400 of the Common Era. He especially taught that all things arise from the mind. He wrote many commentaries. The writings of both Nagarjuna and Vasubandhu are still widely read today.

About the seventh century of the Common Era, a new kind of Buddhism began to be important. It is called Vajrayana, which means the Diamond Vehicle. Vajrayana teaches the importance of attitudes connected with ceremonies. Ceremonies create a special frame of mind. This frame of mind helps men to get rid of desire. So Vajrayana has many ceremonies that are important to its followers.

From the eight century on, there were many changes in India. The Moslems began to conquer India. Wars went on and on. The middle class began to disappear because of wars and changes in society. The majority of Buddhists were middle class. Therefore, Buddhism, too, began to disappear. By the end of the twelfth century Buddhism was almost gone in India. It hung on in some country districts.

When the British arrived in India, there were few Buddhists. Some Buddhists communities still lived on in Bengal. Others continued in Ladakh. But there were very few Buddhists. In the end of the nineteenth century, a revival of Buddhism started. Dharmapala, a man from Ceylon, began to preach Buddhism in India. He started the Mahabodhi Society. This is a great missionary society. It has started mission work in many countries. But its most important work is in India. The Mahabodhi Society runs orphanages, temples, and schools in India. It won back to Buddhist ownership many of the great Buddhist temples built by Asoka and other kings in olden times. It won to Buddhism millions of modern Indians.

Questions (to be answered in writing)

1. Why was Subhadra glad? 2. What could be done by the monks now that the Buddha was dead? 3. Why was Kasyapa sad? 4. What did Kasyapa suggest? 5. What did one monk say after the sutras had been memorized by groups of the five hundred monks? 6. What happened because many other monks memorized what they themselves had heard from the Buddha? 7. Who was told some rules could be changed? 8. Which rules for the monks could be changed after the Buddha's death? 9. What is one reasonable example of a needed change? 10. Who was Asoka? 11. Where were the words of Asoka written? 12. Who was Kanishka? 13. What did Kanishka have the sutras written on? 14. How did Asvaghosa spread Buddhism? 15. What does Mahayana mean? 16. What does Hinayana mean? 17. What is the chief difference between Mahayana and Hinayana? 18. Who are the two greatest Mahayana teachers? 19. When did Nagarjuna live? 20. What especial truth did he emphasize? 21. When did Vasubandhu live? 22. What truth did Vasubandhu especially emphasize? 23. What form of Buddhism arose to importance about the seventh century? 24. What does the word Vajrayana mean? 25. What does Vajrayana emphasize especially? 26. What happened to the middle class in India after the eighth century? 27. What effect did the changes in the Middle Class have on Buddhism? 28. What happened in Indian Buddhism at the end of the nineteenth century? 29. Who led the revival? 30. What is the Mahabodhi Society?

THE BUDDHIST SCRIPTURES

When Sakyamuni died, his disciples gathered together for a great conference. At this conference the disciples recited together the teachings of the Buddha. Ananda, of course, had long been the personal attendant of Sakyamuni Buddha, so Ananda was questioned as to what he had heard from the lips of the Buddha. To each question, he began: "Thus have I heard. Once the Buddha dwelt at . . . " To this day all sutras begin with these words. There were other disciples who recited the rules of discipline, which are called vinaya; the vinaya is the rules for monks and nuns. Still a third group of scriptures was put together, as well; it was a collection of discussions of philosophy, psychology, and metaphysics. These three groups of scriptures were handed down orally for hundreds of years, and even today many clerics have memorized large portions of the scriptures, which they can recite in the ancient manner.

The three groups sutras, vinaya, and discussions—are called the Three Baskets. The scriptures preserved in the Pali language alone are about thirty volumes. This many more can still be found in Sanskrit. Pali and Sanskrit are two ancient languages of India. They are related to Latin, Greek, and other languages of Europe. Pali and Sanskrit are closely related. They have many words that are exactly alike. Other words are very similar. Dharma is Sanskrit and the Pali form is Dhamma. Nirvana is Sanskrit and Nibbana is Pali. In writing about Buddhism in English, words are often borrowed from Pali or Sanskrit. There is no strict rule as to which language should be borrowed. In the same way, both languages were used by Buddhists in ancient India. Both Sanskrit and Pali were used to write the scriptures. But, with the murder of monks and nuns in wars and religious persecutions, many scriptures were lost in these languages. Many scriptures which were lost in Pali or Sanskrit are still found in Tibetan and Chinese versions. Translations into Chinese and Tibetan were begun early when there were still many Buddhists in India.

In China and Tibet many commentaries and explanations

were also translated from Indian languages. Chinese and Tibetan monks also wrote many commentaries on the sutras and other scriptures. With time, these, too, were published along with the Three Baskets. Thus the size of the scriptures grew in China, Tibet, and later in Japan; moreover, the distinction of the Three Baskets became obscure. Thus, in China and Japan the whole unified body of Buddhist scriptures is called the *Great Thesaurus of Scriptures* (dai-zo-kyo).

If this *Great Thesaurus of Scriptures* were translated into English, it would require nearly four hundred books the size of the Encyclopedia Britannica to print one set. About ten percent has been translated into Western languages.

With such a huge body of scriptures certain problems arise. Clearly the Buddhist "Bible" cannot be carried to Sunday school. It is even difficult for the learned clergy to read it all the way through. However, we know that Honen read through the whole Thesaurus, and Shinran is said to have been the proofreader for the publication of one edition of it. Most people, however, never attempt to read the whole body of Buddhist scriptures.

The clergy, of course, use many portions of the scriptures. In his *Teaching, Practice, Faith and Attainment,* Shinran quotes from nearly forty sutras and commentaries. In his other writings he quotes from many others.

The tremendous size of the Thesaurus, however, has led to a strange situation. It seems that different sects use different "Bibles." If you look at the scripture books most commonly used by the sects of Japan, they do not all contain the same sutras and commentaries. The founders of each sect selected out of the Thesaurus those works which he felt his followers could understand. He talked about these, wrote commentaries on them, and handed them down. Zen alone says it is not founded on a scripture; but this, it should be understood, does not mean Zen rejects the Buddhist scriptures. Zen means it is not founded on one scripture: it means that it is based upon the whole Thesaurus of Scriptures without emphasizing a special one. Other sects, however, do emphasize some parts of the Thesaurus over others; but they all accept and every work in the whole of the Buddhist canon as a true and proper scripture. Shin Buddhism publishes a collection of sutras and discussions, together with sectarial commentaries on these. This might be called the Sectarial canon. It is not used in place of the Thesaurus, but in addition to it. The most commonly used collection today in the Honganji tradition is *The Complete Writings of the Sacred Scriptures of the True Teachings* (Shinshu Shogyo Zensho). This is in five volumes. Among the most important works it contains are the following:

1. *The Sutra Spoken by the Buddha on Endless Life* (Bus-setsu-mu-ryo-ju-kyo).

2. *The Sutra Spoken by the Buddha on the Insight of Endless Life* (Bus-setsu—kan-muryo-ju-kyo).

3. *The Sutra Spoken by the Buddha on Amida* (Bus-setsu-a-mi-da-kyo).

These three are the main scriptures of the Shin sect. The following writings, in a sense, are all commentaries on these three sutras. Some of the following are prose, some poetry.

9. *The Chapter on the Simple Practice* (I-gyo-bon) and

10. *The Twelve Obeisances* (Ju-ni-rai) are by Nagarjuna.

11. *The Treatise on the Pure Realm* (Jo-do-ron) is written by Vasubandhu.

12. *The Annotations of the Treatise on the Pure Realm* (O-jo-ron-chu).

13. *The Song in Praise of Amida Buddha* (San-a-mi-da-butsu-ge).

14. *An Abbreviated Treatise on the Principle of the Pure Realm and Happiness* (Ryaku-ron-an-raku-jo-do-gi) are written by Donran in Chinese.

15. *The Anthology on Peace and Happiness* (An-raku-shu) was written by Doshaku.

16. *Four Books of Annotations on the Insight Sutra* (Kan-gyo-shi-jo-sho);

17. *Praises of Matters of the Law* (Ho-ji-san);

18. *The Entrance to the Law by the Thought of Insight* (Kan-nen-bo-mon);

19. *A Song of Praise and Acknowledgement of Rebirth* (O-jo-rai-san-ge); and

20. *Pratyut Praises* (Han-ju-san) were written by the Chinese Zendo.

21. *Anthology of the Essentials on Rebirth* (O-jo-yo-shu) were written in Chinese by the Japanese Genshin.

22. *An Anthology on the Thought of the Buddha in the Selected Main Vow* (Sen-jaku-hon-gan-nem-butsu-shu) was written in Chinese by Shinran's teacher Genku-Honen.

23. *The Teaching, Practice, Faith, and Attainment* (Kyo-gyo-shin-sho) is Shinran's chief explanation of his teachings. This book is written in Chinese, the Latin of the Far East.

28. (Japanese) *Praises of the Pure Realm* (Jo-do-wa-san).

29. (Japanese) *Praises of the Eminent Frairs* (Ko-so-wa-san).

30. (Japanese) *Praises of the Period of the True, Semblence and Latter Law* (Sho-zo-matsu-wa-san). These three books are collections of Shinran's poems. These poems are written in simple Japanese, and sum up the history of Buddhism as well as give a good outline of his own teachings.

50. *The Notes Lamenting Differences* (Tan-i-sho)
This is a very popular explanation of Shinran's teachings; it was written by a disciple, but his name has been lost. There are a dozen translations into English, and it has been translated into a number of other languages as well.

71. *The Espistles* (Go-bun-sho)
were written by Rennyo, eighth generation descendant of Shinran. These letters were written in simple Japanese to his followers, and they were collected into a book. They formed a kind of correspondence course on Shin Buddhism.

74. *The Confession of the Received Understanding* (Ryo-ge-mon) is often called in English *The Creed*. There are many translations of this into English.

77. *The Notes on his Holy Life* (Go-den-sho)
is a biography of Shinran; it was written by Kakunyo, his great-grandson and is used in ceremonies each January when it is read over seven nights in temple. There are English translations.

We have listed, of course, only a few of the hundreds of works in the Complete Writings. But these are important books, and every Shin follower should know their names, at least.

The day is still far in the future when all these five volumes will be available in English. Little by little, however, they are being translated.

Questions (to be answered in writing)

1. What did the disciples do when Sakyamuni died? 2. Who had been Sakyamuni's personal attendant? 3. About what was Ananda questioned? 4. Why do all sutras begin with the words "Thus have I heard"? 5. How many divisions or groups of scriptures were made? 6. How were the scriptures handed down? 7. What are the three divisions of the scriptures? 8. What name is given to the three divisions as a collection? 9. Why are not the same scriptures found today in all the chief languages of Buddhism? 10. How were many commentaries added to the Buddhist canon? 11. What does the word canon mean? 12. What is the *Great Thesaurus of Scriptures?* 13. How large is the Buddhist canon? 14. Why do different sects use different scriptures? 15. What are the names of the chief sutras used by the Shin sect? 16. Who wrote the *Twelve Obeisances?* 17. What is Shinran's chief book? 18. What is the chief collection of Rennyo's teachings? 19. What is the Ryo-ge-mon? 20. What is the chief biography of Shinran?

JAPANESE BUDDHISM

a. Early Buddhism in Japan

About one thousand years after the death of Sakyamuni, a Korean king sent Buddhist scriptures and images to Japan. He said that the Buddha was honored the world over. He urged the Japanese to accept Buddhism. The Mononobe clan, who were the guardians of the military, told the Japanese Emperor to destroy these gifts. But the Soga family, who were the chief civilian leaders, wanted to allow people to practice Buddhism. The Emperor sided with the Mononobe family. He refused to have anything to do with Buddhism. A generation later, however, the Korean king tried again. This time he sent not only scriptures and images but clergy as well. After some unpleasantness between the Mononobe and the Soga family, the monks were allowed to stay in Japan.

Buddhism was first adopted by the Japanese nobility. Many centuries passed before it seeped down to the common people. At the beginning of the seventh century Suiko, a woman, reigned as Emperor. Her Regent or prime minister was Prince Shotoku. He was a devout Buddhist. Shotoku was the greatest of Japanese laymen, and one of the great men of all times. During his time full religious freedom was given to Japanese Buddhism for the first time. Shotoku himself wrote commentaries on three Buddhist scriptures, and he lectured to the Emperor on Buddhism. During this period a number of temples were built. A system of temples was also started, so that Buddhism might be taught in all the provinces.

The early monks taught the arts of road-making and bridge-building and farming as well as Buddhism. Monastic students were included in the embassies to China, so that they could study Buddhist doctrine and culture in the great monasteries there.

Between the middle of the seventh century and the middle of the eighth, the influence of China upon Japan grew greatly. Six Buddhist schools were introduced from China. Later Japanese Buddhism says two of these schools to be imperfect and Hinayanist. However, this is the prejudiced view of later times. It cannot be admitted in an objective view of the history of the period. The imperfection of these schools is entirely relative to one's acceptance or rejection of their teachings. Neither are they strictly Hinayanist; indeed, at most, they accepted a Hinayanistic tradition. Their doctrines are largely changed from those of primitive

Buddhism. They are, for the most part, not based on the Pali canon or its equivalent.

Only from the eighth century has Japan had a permanent capital; until the later part of the nineteenth century, this capital was at what is now called Kyoto. Until the establishment of a permanent capital, native Buddhist scholarship made little progress. Most of the teachers were Chinese or Korean. A permanent capital, however, allowed for stability and continuity in the teaching of Buddhism. For there was now greater assurance that the temples would continue to be the center of the nation's activities. This economic, political, and cultural stability especially benefited two great religious leaders who arose at the end of the eighth century. One of these was Saicho, later known as Dengyo Daishi. The other was Kukai, who is better known as Kobo Daishi.

Both Dengyo and Kobo had been sent to study in China. At this time, a great eclectic movement was underway in Chinese Buddhism. For several centuries Buddhist scriptures and commentaries had been in the process of translation into Chinese. The translation work was almost on a mass production basis. Translated out of a dozen languages or more, a large quantity of Buddhist literature had been amassed in Chinese. The Chinese Buddhists, however, found it impossible to understand all these doctrinally and historically. A number of eclectic movements arose. These tried to make sense and order out of the Chinese Buddhist canon. This canon or collection of scriptures is several hundred times the size of the Bible or the Koran.

A number of systems were developed for assigning each sutra to some period in Sakya's life. Each system then viewed the whole canon as leading up to some particular final revelation of the real and essential truth of Buddhism just before his death. One of the most influential of these systems was that developed by Chih-k'ai at Mount T'ien-t'ai in the Chinese province of Chakiang. He regarded the whole of Sakya's teaching a leading up to the preaching of the *Lotus of the Pure Law Sutra.*

It is this doctrine of the *Lotus Sutra* as the perfection of

Buddhist teaching which Dengyo carried back to Japan. He carried on the eclectic teachings by harmonizing and including within Buddhism, Shinto, the native primitive religion of ancient Japan. Moreover, he started a new ordination platform. On the grounds that the Japanese were already so good and pure that they did not need the Vinaya discipline, Dengyo started a new "Bodhisattva-discipline." This completely abandoned the Hinayanistic rules for monks which had been handed down earlier.

Another eclectic system was brought back to Japan by Kobo. In China he was initiated into the esoteric school then fashionable there. Though this esoteric school virtually died out later in China, it became important in Japan as the Shingon school. Kobo, upon his return, made Mount Koya the center of his teachings. There he taught his mystical ritual and doctrines.

The following three hundred years or so were devoted to the scholastic study of Buddhist doctrines. During this period, Buddhism slowly sifted down to the common people. As the centuries passed, the common people increasingly organized for themselves lecture-meetings where they chanted Buddhist litanies and learned Buddhist doctrine. The tenth and eleventh centuries were a period of almost constant civil war, and this turmoil much weakened the older Buddhist sects. Moreover, it strengthened the idea that the world was now entering the period of the Latter Law when Buddhism was to begin a long slow decline.

Questions (to be answered in writing)
1. How long after Sakyamuni's death was it before Buddhism came to Japan? 2. From what country was Buddhism introduced to Japan? 3. What class of people first adopted Buddhism in Japan? 4. What was Shotoku's attitude toward Buddhism? 5. How many schools or sects were introduced from China to Japan? 6. What sutra is the basis of the T'ien't'ai (Tendai) teaching? 7. What sect did Dengyo bring to Japan? 8. What does the word "eclectic" mean? 9. What discipline did Dengyo introduce

into Japan? 10. What does the word "esoteric" mean? 11. What teachings did Kobo bring from China? 12. What was the center from which Kobo's teaching spread in Japan? 13. Who attended the lecture-meetings of Japan? 14. When did lecture-meetings originate?

b. Mediaeval Buddhism

Out of the difficulties of war, famine, and plague, arose the first independent Japanese schools of Buddhism. The first important Japanese school is the Jodo Sect. It was established in 1153, by Genku-Honen. Honen's main teaching was that since the people were living in the period of the Latter Law they were not able to live any of the hard rules of Buddha. People had but one hope of liberation or "salvation." The only hope of these people, Honen taught, was to be born in the Pure Realm of Amida Buddha. Here they could more easily attain Enlightenment. The key to rebirth lay in the calling of the Name and Title of Amida Buddha. This calling is one of the ten practices of the bodhisattva (seeker of Enlightenment). Honen, however, insisted this act of praising Buddha was alone good enough to bring about rebirth into the Pure Realm.

About the time that Honen was first becoming famous, Eisai, a Japanese monk, returned from China with Rinzai-Zen. This is one of the three main branches of Japanese Zen. The other two are Soto, which was introduced by Dogen in 1223, and Obaku, introduced by the Chinese monk Lung-ch'i, in 1650. Zen, which emphasizes meditation, says its teachings are a special transmission of the essence of Sakya's teachings, and that it is a transmission outside the scriptures. Rinzai, in fact, stresses its transmission from heart to heart without words. Soto, however, emphasizes scholarship and research in addition to meditation. Zen is a development of Buddhism which grew out of the effort to teach Buddhism to Chinese farmers. In Japan, it became the religion of professional soldiers.

At the time Zen was being introduced by Eisai and Dogen, Shinran, a disciple of Honen, was preaching his own understanding of his master's message. Shinran taught that in the egolessness of the moment of faith the efficient cause was created for the attainment of complete enlightenment at the instant of death. In the following generation, the Shin school was organized out of Shinran's disciples. This organization slowly developed into a Buddhist sect. For generations the Shin sect has been the most influential of all forms of Japanese Buddhism. It has started foreign missions in Russia, Korea, China, Malaya, the Philippines, the South Sea islands, Hawaii, Brazil, Canada, the United States, Germany and Austria.

About this same time, the last of the three really important native Japanese formations of Buddhism came into existence. This is the Hokke school. It was formed around the teachings of Nichiren. He lived from 1222 to 1282. Nichiren took as the center of his teachings the *Lotus of the Pure Law Sutra.* He tried to reform the Japanese Tendai school. He opposed the eclecticism of that school. Thinking the Sakya of the *Lotus of the Pure Law* was the only true Buddha, Nichiren urged a return to obedience to this Buddha alone. In making this proclamation, Nichiren thought himself to be Visistacaritra Bodhisattva. The *Lotus Sutra* says that in the beginning of the days of the Latter Law this bodhisattva would teach the Buddha's true teachings.

The following three centuries were a very unsettled era in Japanese history. During this period a number of minor lords were struggling for leadership. Many of the monasteries became military camps, and a class of military clerics arose who, wearing armor and wielding swords, fought in secular causes. It should be understood, however, that these soldier-clerics were never concerned with religious disputes. Their interests were entirely secular, and they were not trying to dominate Japan but to create a religious state. The power of the soldier-clerics was not exercised on behalf of religious convictions.

Japanese Buddhism, of course, has had its full share of sectarian doctrinal controversies, but to the credit of Buddhism it can be recorded that the stake and the rack never found a place among its instruments of self-assertion.

Questions (to be answered in writing)

1. What is the first important Japanese school of Buddhism? 2. Who established the first important Japanese Buddhist sect? 3. What was the chief practice of the Jodo Sect? 4. Who transmitted Rinzai-Zen to Japan? 5. Who introduced Soto-Zen to Japan? 6. When was Obaku-Zen introduced to Japan? 7. For whom was Zen designed in China? 8. Of what class did Zen become the religion in Japan? 9. According to Shinran what is the efficient cause for the attainment of complete enlightenment? 10. What is considered the last of the important native Japanese sects of Buddhism? 11. Did the Buddhist clerics try to make religion dominate government?

c. The Modern Period

With the appearance of the powerful Tokugawa family about 1600, Japan entered into three hundred years of internal peace. This period, however, was one of totalitarian government under the direction of the Tokugawa, acting in the name of the Emperor. Even Buddhism was under the strict regulations laid down by the government. No new doctrines or sects were allowed to be started, and the Buddhists devoted their time to scholarship and religious practice.

About the middle of the seventeenth century, however, a strong revival of the primitive Shinto religion was started. From the ninth century when Buddhism absorbed Shinto, the two had become so closely interwoven in most sects that their separation seemed hopeless. Under the influence of the Shinto revival, however, a new Shinto doctrine was invented in opposition to Buddhism.

The principles of this new Shinto became the basis of the restoration of 1867, when the Emperor began to rule himself. Shinto rites and rituals were adopted by the government. Buddhism was virtually outlawed. But Buddhism had twined its roots too deeply around the heart of the people to be thus easily torn up. It gradually recovered much of its former place, though not its former magnificence, for the anti-Buddhist policies of the Meiji government robbed it of a large part of its income. Moreover, the government openly and officially continued to foster the Shinto revival. This directly weakened the position of Buddhism, especially among the younger generation.

During the Second World War the Japanese Government again outlawed Buddhism. After the War, the United Nations' Occupation policies went on to work against Buddhism. Though finally freedom of religion was guaranteed, the new post-war administration confiscated nearly all temple lands, so many sects became very poor.

Moreover, a new religion corporate-body law upset twenty-five centuries of Buddhist traditional system. It caused temples to be reorganized upon the congregationalist patterns of United States' Protestantism. However, the most serious effect from this new law has been, in most sects, a complete breakdown of church order. The number of Buddhist sects has grown to several hundred. Much of this separatism is admittedly due to personal vanity.

Most of these "sects" have but a single temple. However, there is no such thing as an "independent" temple, and some of the new "sects" ought rather to be considered simply independent temples. In a number of such cases, there is very valid reason to regard these temples as historically and economically independent and non-sectarian. Doctrinally, of course, their teachings may be, and frequently are, a thousand or more years old. Often their buildings are eleven or twelve centuries old; it is their organized systems alone which are new.

Questions (to be answered to writing)

1. What family ruled Japan for nearly three hundred years after 1600? 2. What kind of government did Japan have during the Tokugawa era? 3. To what did Buddhists devote most of their attention in the Tokugawa era? 4. What native religion had a revival about this time? 5. What happened to Buddhism at the Restoration? 6. What has been the attitude of the Japanese government towards Buddhism after 1867? 7. What happened to Buddhist organization and discipline during the Occupation? 8. Why are there so many new "sects" in post-war Japan?

SHINRAN OF THE HONGANJI

Shinran of the Honganji was born in the suburbs of Kyoto, the Japanese capital, in 1173 of the Common Era. His father, Arinori, a member of the Hino family of the Fujiwara clan, was First Secretary to the Empress Dowager. His mother was a descendant of the Emperor Seiwa.

The loss of both parents when Shinran was still a child, led him to enter religion. Accompanied by his uncle, the nine-year old child asked permission to become an acolyte of a distant relative, Jien-Jichin. Jien-Jichin was one of the greatest Buddhist clerics of the day.

The eminent abbot would have delayed the tonsure until the morrow. However, the child, in a brilliantly improvised verse, reminded him that the future is uncertain, and so Jien-Jichin agreed to give him tonsure that very evening.

As the young acolyte progressed, he was sent to study on Mt. Hiei in the Northern Range. Here he remained for some years to penetrate all the teachings of Buddhism; but somehow religious awakening eluded him.

Seeking a deeper religious experience, the earnest young friar made a pilgrimage for one hundred nights to the Rokkaku-do (Hexagonal Chapel) in the Imperial Capital.

Near the end of the hundred nights, he chanced to make the acquaintance of Honen, a celebrated teacher, who answered many of the questions which troubled Shinran's heart. Accordingly, he became a disciple of Honen and, taking the name Zenshin, dwelt with his master at Yoshimizu (Blessed Waters) on the outskirts of the capital.

Studying earnestly under Honen, Zenshin soon became one of the leading disciples at Yoshimizu. He was given the privilege of painting his Master's portrait and copying Honen's own copy of the Master's *Anthology on the Thought of the Buddha in the Selected Main Vow.*

On one occasion, Honen's disciples were debating an important point in their Master's teachings and the majority, who supported one interpretation gathered on one side of the hall, while the few opponents, among whom was Shinran, gathered on the other. When Honen himself was asked to choose the correct side, he stepped over to Shinran and the two or three disciples who supported him.

The outspoken criticism of the nationalistic Shinto cult by the group at Yoshimizu, as well as the rising fear caused by the group's strength, led the government to find an excuse to exile Honen and his disciples for treason for insulting the Emperor.

Zenshin was forced to return to lay status and exiled to the remote wilderness of North Japan. Here, however, he rejoiced at the opportunity to spread the teachings of Buddha among the forgotten country folk.

When at last his term of exile was commuted, he wished to rejoin his Master at once. But before he could set out on his return to the capital, word came of the death of Honen. Shinran cancelled his return and later moved to the remote east.

In the province of Hitachi, Shinran married and lived for many years. He spent much of his time composing a treatise in Chinese on Buddhism as he understood it, and in teaching his friends and neighbors.

Shinran's success in teaching and his honored position in

the community aroused considerable jealousy. An assassin once sought to kill him, but, on coming face to face with Shinran, the assassin was so impressed that he became the saint's disciple.

At sixty, Shinran retired to the capital to die in the familiar surroundings of his youth. Shinran's life continued thirty years, however, and he devoted himself in this period to teaching and writing of Buddhism in the simple language of the people.

In 1262, attended by a few friends and disciples, the saintly Shinran died. Though he had asked his friends to throw his body as food to the fishes of the Kamo river, he was cremated and his remains buried at Ohtani, on the Higashiyama (Eastern Mountain), outside the capital.

His youngest daughter took charge of his grave, and shortly a small mausoleum was built. This was soon recognized as a temple, and Shinran's disciples and friends came here on pilgrimages to express their gratitude for the teachings of Buddha which Shinran had made known to them.

Questions (to be answered in writing)

1. In what year was Shinran of the Honganji born? 2. Of what clan was Shinran? 3. What was Shinran's family name? 4. What was Shinran's father, Arinori? 5. Of whom was Shinran's mother a descendant? 6. When did Shinran's parents die? 7. With whom did Shinran go to seek ordination? 8. What does the word acolyte mean? 9. Who was Jien-Jichin? 10. What does tonsure mean? 11. What did Abbot Jien-Jichin want to delay? 12. What did the child remind the Abbot? 13. How did the child remind the Abbot? 14. What does improvised mean? 15. To what mountain was Shinran sent to study? 16. Did Shinran study all the teachings of Buddhism? 17. What does penetrate mean? 18. Did Shinran attain awakening on Mount Hiei? 19. To what chapel did Shinran go for one hundred nights? 20. Whom did Shinran meet near the end of the hundred nights? 21. What name did Shinran take when he became Honen's disciple? 22. Where did Shinran

live with Honen? 23. What incident showed that Shinran truly understood Honen's teaching? 24. Why were Honen and his disciples exiled? 25. What happened to Zenshin-Shinran? 26. Why did Shinran not return to the capital? 27. In what language did Shinran write an important book? 28. What happened when an assassin tried to kill Shinran? 29. At what age did Shinran return to the capital? 30. What did Shinran do for the last thirty years of his life? 31. In what year did Shinran die? 32. What did Shinran want done with his body after he had died? 33. What was done with his corpse? 34. Where was Shinran buried? 35. What was built at his grave? 36. Why did Shinran's disciples and friends come to his mausoleum?

THE SHIN SECT

Our denomination is called by many names. It is most correctly called the Jodo-shinshu. Jodo means "Pure Land" or "Pure Realm". Shinshu means "true teaching". In modern Japanese, the work "-shu" has come also to mean "sect" or denomination. Thus, Shinshu is sometimes called the Shin Sect or even the True Sect.

As a sect Shin started in Japan. But the teachings were very old. They go back to China and to India. When we say these are a true teaching, we do not mean other forms of Buddhism are false. The teachings handed down from Shinran are a true teaching. They are not the only true teaching.

Shinran did not try to start a sect or denomination. He taught his friends and neighbors. They all thought themselves disciples of Buddha. They met regularly together to hear preaching. Usually they met in homes, but sometimes they gathered in the halls of neighborhood temples where they could borrow a room. During Shinran's life, they met each month on the day that Honen had died. After Shinran died, they met on the day of his death.

After Shinran's death, these friends and neighbors often visited his grave. They came to express their gratitude for the joy and happiness they had from his teachings. Shinran's grave was tended by his daughter at first. Later, his great-grandson Kakunyo was placed in charge. A small chapel was built at Shinran's grave, and it was given the name Honganji, which means Temple of the Main Vow.

Shinran's disciples were called monto, which means "Fellows at the gate". The groups of his disciples slowly organized themselves into fellowships. So sometimes outsiders call our sect the Montoshu or Sect of Fellowships.

If they were already Buddhist when they joined Shinran's disciples, the fellows did not leave the sect they were connected with. Most of these members belonged to the Tendai Sect. In addition to their activities in their original sect, they met each month to hear about Buddhism as Shinran understood it.

Some of Shinran's disciples were quite learned. Some were good speakers and teachers. These people naturally became the leaders of their fellowships. Often branch fellowships were started, and rather large groups developed.

Ten fellowships, in time, came to be the most important. These slowly developed into schools and sects. A few became independent only in the late nineteenth century. These ten fellowships developed into the ten Branches of the Shin Sect. Each is independent. Each teaches Shinran's doctrines. Each has many branch temples.

The ten Branches are all said to be correct and true. They all teach Shinran's doctrines carefully and correctly. If a member or a cleric wants to change his membership from one Branch to another, he just tells an officer in his sect. Then all his records are transferred to the new branch he wants to join. All ten Branches spread the True Teaching about the Pure Realm just as Shinran taught it. Each Branch is a true sect.

These ten Branches have their headquarters in different parts of Japan. The main Honganji (Hompa Honganji) has its headquarters at Nishi Honganji Temple in Kyoto. The Otani Branch also has its headquarters in Kyoto at its chief temple which is called Higashi Honganji. The Takada Branch headquarters is in Senshuji Temple at Isshinden, some miles from Nagoya. The Kosho Branch has its headquarters at Koshoji Temple, which is just next door to the Nishi Honganji in Kyoto. The Bukkoji Branch has its headquarters at Chuzu Township in Shiga Prefecture near Kyoto. These are the six main branches of the Shin sect. Each of these larger Branches has, in modern times, started foreign missions. Each of these Branches has tried to spread Shin beyond the boundaries of Japan.

There are four smaller Branches. They have fewer members and not so well known, but they too trace themselves back to Shinran's disciples. They are the Izumoji Branch, the Joshoji Branch, the Yamamoto Branch, and the Sammonto Branch.

These ten Branches of the Shin Sect invite each other's clergy to teach in their temples. Most of their clerics attend the same universities and seminaries. They are not rivals. They are all fellow-believers in the teachings of Buddha as these were handed down through Shinran of the Honganji.

Questions (to be answered in writing)
1. What does the Japanese word Shinshu mean in English?
2. What meaning has been added to "-shu" in modern Japanese?
3. Are Shinran's teachings the only true teachings of Buddhism?
4. Where did the teachings of Shin originate as an organized sect?
5. Does Shinran's teaching go back to Buddha? 6. Did Shinran try to start a denomination? 7. Where did the early Shin believers meet? 8. On what day each month did the believers meet after Shinran died? 10. Why did people visit Shinran's grave? 11. What was the name of the chapel built at Shinran's grave? 12. What does Honganji mean in English? 13. What does "fellow" mean?

14. What does "fellowship" mean? 15. What were Shinran's disciples called? 16. What were the congregations of Shinran's disciples called? 17. Why is our sect sometimes called Montoshu? 18. When people joined a Shin fellowship, did they leave their former sect? 19. How many Branches of Shin Sect developed? 20. Are some of the ten Branches of the Shin Sect false? 22. What are the six larger Branches of the Shin Sect? 23. Can members and clerics transfer from one Branch to another?

THE HONGANJI

Each of the ten branches of the Shin sect is headed by a Good Teacher-Friend (zen-ji-shiki) who inherits his office from his father or uncle. He is known by a variety of titles. These titles include Patriarch (hos-shu), Porter (mon-shu) and Master. In English, he is sometimes called Abbot or Lord Abbot. But he is not a monk, so this title is not proper. From olden times, the patriarchs of most branches of the Shin sect held a court rank equal to a prince. This rank is called, in Japanese, mon-zeki.

The Honganji today is managed by the Patriarch. He is a direct descendant of Shinran. The present Patriarch is Kosho Ohtani.

The Patriarch, however, as the guardian of Shinran's teachings, represents all the members of the denomination. He is directly assisted by the Ecclesiastical Congress (Shu-e). The clergy and lay members select the members of the Congress. The Honganji denomination is directly run by an Administrative Bishop. The Patriarch nominates two or three candidates for this office. The Congress then chooses one by majority vote, and this candidate becomes the chief administrative officer of the Honganji.

The Administrative Bishop (So-cho) chooses a cabinet (so-mu). The members of his cabinet help him in the business of our sect. In addition, he appoints the heads of various departments. The Honganji has several departments that are not just administrative.

These include a Department of Mission and Educational Activities, a Department of Publication, and a Department of Social Welfare.

The Patriarch spends much of his time in traveling to teach about Shin Buddhism, as does his wife, who is called in Japanese ura-kata. He is assisted in doctrinal matters by the Bureau of Scholarchs. This is like the College in Cardinals of the Roman Catholic Church. These Scholarchs represent the highest rank of the Honganji sect.

The ranks of the scholarly clergy are five: Activist (tokugo), Associate in Studies (jo-kyo), Counsellor in Studies (ho-ky0), Director in Studies (shi-kyo), and Scholarch (kan-gaku).

In all, the Honganji sect branch has about 23,000 clerics in nearly 12,000 temples. Well over a hundred of these temples are in Europe and in North and South America. About 15,000 of these clerics held the rank of docent (kyoshi). This rank is required of these who are rectors (head ministers) of temples. In Japan itself there are about five hundred missioners who devote full-time to spreading Shin Buddhism. About two hundred foreign missioners are sent out by the Patriarch to lead congregations in foreign lands.

The Honganji branch has today in Japan about 7 million followers. Of these, about one and a half million represent the increase in members since 1868. They are noted in temple records as believers (shin-to). Five and half million members represent the old original members from before 1868.

Among organizations in Japan sponsored by the Honganji is the Buddhist Ladies Association, with 7500 societies. The Young Buddhist Association has 3500 societies. The Honganji also sponsors more than two thousand Sunday schools. The Honganji also has fifty regular schools and grammar schools. There are also seminaries and Buddhist Training institutions. In the last few years thousands of nursery schools or kindergartens have been started in Honganji temples, for the Japanese school system does not include kindergarten or "pre-school" programs.

The Honganji has more than a thousand facilities devoted to social service including medical clinics, and orphanges. The Honganji clergy have also been the leaders in doing religious work in the prisons of Japan.

Questions (to be answered in writing)
1. How does the head of each branch of the Shin sect come into his office? 2. What does the word "Patriarch" mean? 3. Why is the word "Abbot" not suited to the head of the Honganji? 4. From whom is Kosho Ohtani descended? 5. Is the patriarch of the Honganji an absolute ruler? Why do you answer this way? 6. What does the Ecclesiastical Congress do? 7. What is the meaning of the word "ecclesiastical"? 8. Who runs the business of the Honganji denomination? 9. What is the meaning of "denomination"? 10. How is the Administrative Bishop chosen? 11. What does "administrative" means? 12. What officials are chosen by the Administrative Bishop? 13. For what purpose does the Patriarch travel? 14. Who assists the Patriarch in doctrinal problems? 15. How many academic ranks are there in the Shin clergy? 16. About how many temples in Japan are Shin? 17. On what other continents are there Shin temples? 18. About how many followers belong to the Honganji? 19. How can you tell that the Honganji denomination is still growing? 20. What educational activity is quite new in the Honganji temples?

BUDDHISM IN AMERICA
The earliest historical records of the coming of Buddhism to America are written in Chinese. They tell of monks coming to the Western World in the fifth century of the Common Era. The trip of Hwui-shan carried him along the coast of North America as far as Mexico. His record is accepted by many scholars as an authentic historical record. It can be read in Edward P. Vining's

An Inglorious Columbus; or, Evidence that Hwui Shan and a Party of Buddhist Monks from Afghanistan Discovered America in the Fifth Century, A.D. (New York, 1885).

However, the first known Buddhist in modern times in America is the Shin Sectator Zenmatsu. He came to what is now the state of Hawaii in 1807. Zenmatsu was surprised to hear that the Buddha's teachings were unknown there.

Buddhism was at this time, however, being mentioned in occasional books and magazines in the eastern states. *The Catalogue of the Library of Thomas Jefferson,* for example, shows he had some books referring to Buddhism. He also had a copy of the life of Saint Josephat who, as is well known, is really the Buddha Sakyamuni.

The first American Buddhist seems to have been the well known Henry David Thoreau. His confession of Buddhism is to be seen in the chapter "Sunday" in his *Week on the Concord and Merrimack Rivers,* first published in 1849. Under his influence, too, the famous magazine *Dial* in its fourth volume published an article about Buddha.

Another American Buddhist who had great influence on an oriental land was Ernest Francisco Fenollosa (Feb. 13, 1851—Sept. 21, 1903). Fenollosa was an educator in Japan when things Japanese were out of fashion. He became much interested in Japanese art. He finally was able to get Japan to pass a law protecting important pieces of Japanese art. He helped to build up the great collections of Japanese art in the Boston Museum and wrote much on the traditional arts of Japan. Fenollosa converted to the Tendai Sect of Buddhism. As a Buddhist, he was given the religious name Teishin. He is buried at Mii-dera (see the *Dictionary of American Biography,* 1933).

In 1892 there was in Chicago a great World Congress of Religions. To this came Dharmapala from Ceylon and several clerics from Japan. Dharmapala, fluent in English and well versed in Buddhism, created a sensation. After his lecture before the Congress, he was invited to speak in many places and he converted many people, including Mrs. Mary Foster of Honolulu. This wealthy lady donated the land for the Honganji Betsuin in Honolulu. She also gave hundreds of thousands of dollars to help spread Buddhism in all the world.

In the Seventies, the Eighties, the Njneties, Buddhism became increasingly familiar to Americans. Many books and magazine articles were published telling about Buddhism. Many people took great interest in Buddhist thought. A number of crack-pots and charletans took advantage of this. Some claimed falsely to be Buddhist monks, and most lectured on Buddhism or tried to start Buddhist meditation centers. One of the leaders in the fight against such confidence men was Paul Carus, editor of *The Gospel of Buddha,* and other important books on Buddhism. He was also editor of *The Open Court* magazine. Carus was a close friend of all the important thinkers of the world. One of his books on Buddhism was translated into Russian by his good friend Tolstoy.

In 1853, the *Journal of the American Oriental Society* published a translation of the *Life of Buddha* from Burmese. Though Buddhist were few at this time, Buddhism was recognized as enjoying full freedom in the United States. A Supreme Court decision in Maine noted in 1854 that state law regards " . . . the Buddhist, the Catholic and Quaker, as possessing equal rights." Moreover, in 1859, the Massachusetts Supreme Court noted" . . . our constitution (is) . . . for the protection of all religions—the Buddhist, the Jew, the Christian and the Turk, that all might enjoy unrestricted liberty in their religion . . . "

This freedom of religion was of some importance in securing the opening of Japan. Townsend Harris, the consul who made the Ansei Treaty between the United States and Japan, told the Shogun: "In America the followers of Buddha and the followers of Christ live side by side and on the same level. Nobody harbours any evil design in religious matters, being contented to live in peace and quiet." (See the *Lion's Roar,* vol. ii, no. 2, pp. 24-26). The freedom given Buddhists in the United States convinced the Japanese that our government was not out to destroy Japanese tradition, and so it was a little easier to agree on a final treaty.

By this time, of course knowledge about Buddhism was fairly easy to get, if one wanted it. For example, in 1865, the *New American Cyclopaedia,* (volume 4, pp. 61-70) published a long and excellent article on Buddhist history and doctrine.

In 1873 Henry Steel Olcott went to Ceylon where he converted to Buddhism. He had been a colonel in the American Civil War. He remained most of his life in the Orient. Col. Olcott helped to start many schools in India and Ceylon. He hoped to revive Buddhism in these countries. He designed the first Buddhist flag, which is used in all Buddhist lands today. He also wrote a Buddhist catechism.

During this whole period, Buddhism had a growing influence on Americann thinking. It was of some influence on Christian Science, New Thought, Unity and many other movements. Much of this influence was through the Theosophical Society. The Theosophical Society was founded by Col. Olcott and some friends to be a place where all religions could meet together and discuss in friendship their religious beliefs. It soon had branches throughout the world, and it moved its headquarters to India. The Theosophical Society was an important agent of introduction of Indian and Buddhist thought to ordinary Americans.

Buddhism during these years appeared also in the communities of immigrants from the Far East. In the 1850's and 1860's immigrants from China and Japan began to come to the United States. Among the Chinese especially, Buddhist shrines were found. By the 1890's the number of Japanese in California was very large. Representatives were sent to the Honganji in Kyoto to ask for clergy. the Patriarch of Honganji agreed to send clergymen to the United States. On the sixth of July, 1898, the Reverend Eryu Honda and the Reverend Ejun Miyamoto arrived in San Francisco. On the fourteenth of July, they organized the first Young Buddhist Association. On the second of September, 1898, the Reverend Shuye Sonoda and the Reverend Kakuryo Nishijima arrived as the first full-time permanent missioners. On November 28, 1899, they began their first missionary activities among the Caucasian population of San Francisco. Every Sunday afternoon they lectured in English and a sizable congregation was built up. This aroused some opposition among certain Americans. But the Buddhists were able to conduct successful study classes and start a Caucasian Buddhist society. They published also a magazine, *The Light of Dharma,* beginning early in April, 1901. This, however, was not the first Buddhist magazine published in the United States. A group of Caucasian Buddhists in California published *The Buddhist Ray* from 1888 to 1894.

With the continuing flow into the United States and Hawaii of immigrants, Buddhist temples were built in many places. Temples of many Japanese sects were built, and even today, though the Honganji Branch of the Shin sect has the most followers, there are many others. The Ohtani Branch of the Shin sect, the Nichiren sect, the Jodo sect, the Shingon sect, both the Rinzai and the Soto Branches of the Zen sect, and Kegon sect have been established for many years in the United States. In recent years, some new sects have been introduced, including the Soka Gakkai and Risshu Koseikai, which are revival groups in the Nichiren sect.

From about 1900 on, there was an increasing hostility to Japanese immigration in the United States, particularly in Hawaii and California. During this period, there was some activity against Buddhist. Some white Americans thought Buddhism was connected with Japanese nationalism and Japanese militarism.

When World War II broke out with Japan, most of the clergy were arrested by the American government. Later, of course, all Japanese citizens and American citizens of Japanese ancestry were put in concentration camps. Here they continued their religious activities as best they could, introducing Buddhism into such states as Arkansas. All connection with religious centers in Japan was, of course, impossible during the War.

In 1944, at a meeting in Salt Lake City, the Honganji Mission in the United States was reorganized as the Buddhist Churches of America. This name had been used earlier, for we see it often in books written by Caucasians. The Honganji Mission in Hawaii remained separate. It had been started when Hawaii was still a kingdom.

During the war, two Caucasian ministers, Reverends Goldwater and Hunt, carried on as best they could. Their heroic efforts are still bearing fruit. Even in wartime, some Buddhist ministers were let out of concentration camps. They settled in communities far from the West Coast. Here they built new and strong temples which are still growing, even though most Japanese-Americans have returned to the West.

Questions (to be answered in writing)

1. Who was the first Buddhist to come to America? 2. In what century did he come? 3. Who was the first Shin sectator to come to a part of the U.S.? 4. Who is Saint Josephat (check the old Catholic Encyclopedia!)? 5. Who was Henry David Thoreau? 6. Where does Thoreau proclaim himself a Buddhist? 7. Who was Fenollosa? 8. To what sect did Fenollosa belong? 9. Who was Dharmapala? 10. Who donated the land for the Honolulu Honganji Betsuin? 11. Who was Paul Carus? 12. In what two states did the Supreme Court say Buddhism was equal to Christianity in the U.S.? 13. What were the dates of these decisions? 14. How did Buddhism enter into the negotiations for the first treaty between the U.S. and Japan? 15. What early Encyclopedia in the U.S. has an article about Buddhism? 16. Who was Henry Steel Olcott? 17. What was the original purpose of the Theosophical Society? 18. What two groups of immigrants from the orient brought Buddhism to the U.S.? 19. Who were the first permanent

Buddhist missioners in the U.S.? 20. What is the name of the first American Shin magazine? 21. What was the first American Buddhist magazine? 22. What are some of the Japanese sects introduced to the U.S.? 23. When was BCA organized? 24. What was one of the results of the War as far as the spread of Buddhism is concerned?

TEMPLE MEMBERSHIP

Are you a member of your church? Do you belong to your temple association? You probably think you do, but it is quite possible that you are not directly a member of your temple!

In the United States the growth of Buddhist temples did not follow any of the ancient rules. In Chinese communities in California in the 1850's and 1860's, for instance, there were no true temples. However, Buddhist shrines were placed in many of the Chinese community halls for the benefit of Buddhist. These community halls also allowed Taoist and Confucian devotees to keep their shrines in these halls. Thus, the shrines' affairs were managed in part by the directors of the community center. But among Japanese immigrants the development was different.

In many places the Japanese first started Buddhist societies or Young Buddhist associations to provide religious and social relationships. Soon ladies associations were organized; then, later study groups, choirs, boy-scout troops, and other organizations were started. In each community, the Shin Buddhist organizations grew up to meet local needs, so each developed differently.

People joined these organizations directly. These organizations in turn supported and used the temples for social and religious activities. Each such group had its own treasury, and carried on its own activities. Each held its own services. Thus in most temples, people belonged to some special group. To it they paid their dues and made their donations. To its meetings alone they went. Only a few times a year would they attend a general service on some special occasion at the temple.

Such people thought of themselves as belonging to the temple. But, actually their membership was only in one of the auxiliary groups connected with the temple. At most American temples, the Buddhist association (Bukkyokai) holds a general meeting once or twice a year. All people who pay dues to this association can vote at this meeting. At this yearly meeting the board of directors is elected. Besides these elected directors, each connected organization usually has a representative on the board of directors. This board then runs the affairs of the temple with the advice of the minister.

The membership in the Buddhist association varies with the temple. In many places membership is counted by families. In such a case, one person is listed as a member, representing his whole family. Often this one member represents ten or fifteen people or more. In some temples, membership is held individually. In these temples each person who pays dues is a member and may vote for the board of directors. In other temples, a few persons are members individually, and other persons are included in family memberships. For this reason, it is difficult to say how many Shin Buddhists there are in the United States. Many Buddhists do not actually belong to a temple. This, of course, is especially true of Caucasian Buddhists. But it is true also of many people who belong to YBA's and such organizations. Therefore, they are often not counted at all in trying to count the total number of Buddhists.

Temple membership is important to a true Buddhist. Some religions teach that if you do not belong to a certain church you will go to hell. Buddhism does not teach this kind of doctrine. But it is still important to belong to a temple. Without a temple, supported by its members directly, there is no place to learn Buddha's teaching. Moreover, the temple, rather than organizations or groups, is the center of spreading Buddhism in every

67

country. It provides the clergy and helps to educate new clerics. Therefore, it is not enough to belong only to some connected organization. The temple needs support to teach and spread Buddhism.

In Japan, almost all membership in Buddhist temples was by family until the late nineteenth century. This kind of membership was required by law from the seventeenth century on. In Shin, these members are called fellows in English and monto in Japanese; this word means Fellows at the gate. In modern times, new converts to Shin in Japan are usually enrolled at temples as believers, which are called shinja in Japanese. Few American temples, even in those using Japanese, call their members monto or fellows. This is because most of the issei were monto of some temple in Japan. Many of these people thought they might return to Japan, so they did not transfer their membership.

In old Japan, when a person moved permanently to another town, he usually transferred his membership to a new temple near his new home. In the United States this old tradition is still alive, and people usually join a new temple association when they move.

Questions (to be answered in writing)

1. Did Buddhist temples in the U.S. develop in the same way they did in Asia? 2. Did Chinese Buddhists build temples in early California? 3. Where did Chinese Buddhists worship? 4. Why did Japanese start Buddhist associations? 5. What sort of groups were organized? 6. Did most Japanese belong directly to a temple in this country? 7. What does Bukkyokai mean? 8. How is the board of directors usually elected. 9. How are auxiliary organizations represented on the Board of Directors? 10. How is membership held in a temple? 11. Are all Buddhists counted in listing temple membership? 12. Why should a person be a full member of a temple? 13. What does monto mean? 14. Why are members of local temples usually not monto? 15. What does a Shin Buddhist do with his membership when he moves permanently?

THE FEASTS OF THE SHIN HOLY YEAR

Shin Buddhism celebrates a number of special holy days each year. Each of the ten branches sets up its own religious calendar. The holy or feast days celebrated at the main temple and at the sub-temples in each branch are not necessarily the same. There are a number of ceremonies which are only done at the main temple. Some ceremonies have fallen into disuse in many American temples.

Every sub-temple of the Honganji must have a morning and an evening service every day. Even in Japan, however, these are often attended only by the clergy. Each month a special memorial service for Shinran is held on the evening of the 15th, the morning of the 16th, and the noon of this day. Of course, on these days, regular morning and evening services serve this purpose. Each month, for the most part, there is a memorial service for the past Patriarchal Masters, for a service is held in whatever month they might have died.

The chief holy days are fixed. The first holy day of the year is on January first; it is called the Assembly of the First Day (Gan-tan-e, or Shu-sho-e). On this day Shin Buddhists assemble in the temple to rejoice at reaching a new year. They dedicate themselves anew to the teachings of Buddha through the new year.

Perhaps the most important service of the year at the Honganji headquarters comes in the middle of January. It reaches its climax on January 15th and 16th. The service, however, begins a week earlier and is held daily and nightly until a final service on the sixteenth. In branch temples, however, this Proper Memorial (Go-sho-ki) is usually three or five days in length. In some temples this service is only one day long. Only one or two temples traditionally celebrate this feast day in exactly the same way as the Honganji. For on this feast each year, people flock to the Honganji in Kyoto to celebrate in the great temple there. This feast is properly called the Service of the Lecture-Meeting for Thanksgiving and Gratitude (Ho-on-ko-ho-yo). It gives Shin followers an opportunity to express their gratitude for having heard the teachings of Buddha as handed down through Shinran of the Honganji. Because people go from all the world to take part in the services at the Honganji in Kyoto, many temples in Japan have their local services in the late fall rather than in January. However, these temples then have a small service in January also.

On March 7 of each year most Shin temples celebrate the Assembly for the Great Master Enko (En-ko-dai-shi-e). This service expresses gratitude to Honen (also called the Great Master Enko) who was Shinran's teacher-friend.

In March and in September of each year Shin temples celebrate the Vernal and Autumnal Equinoctal Assembly (hi-gan). Its main day is the equinox of spring and fall. The equinox is the day when daylight and night's darkness are exactly the same length. The Equinoctal Assembly is celebrated for seven days, with three days before and three days after the equinox being important. The Equinoctal Assembly originated in Japan and has no history in China or India. It began about 600 C.E. in what is now Osaka. The common people and the clergy would then gather in the main gate of the Temple of the Four Kings of Heaven (Shi-ten-o-ji). There they would meditate on Amida Buddha and his Pure Realm according to the methods of the Sutra of Meditation on Amida Buddha (Kan-gyo). From this habit, the practice spread through the centuries.

In Japan on March 21 also is held a service called the Assembly of the Prince of the Upper Palace (Jo-gu-dai-shi-e). This is a service to remember the work of Prince Shotoku, who established Buddhism as a legal religion in Japan. He wrote Buddhist commentaries, issued a Constitution for Japan, and tried to practice Buddhism as he governed Japan.

On April 15 many Shin temples hold the Service in Commemoration of the Unfolding of our Teaching (Kai-shu-ki-nen-ho-yo). This notes the establishment of the Shin Sect, through the writing of Shinran's *Teaching, Practice, Faith and Attainment.*

The next important service of the year is on May 21. It is the Assembly on the Descent in Birth of the Founder of Our

Teaching (Shu-so-tan-jo-e), but it is more commonly called the Assembly of the Holy Birth (Go-tan-e). In recent years, more particularly in the United States it has been called the Wisteria Festival (Fuji-matsuri). It marks, of course, the birthday of Shinran of the Honganji.

One of the most important holy days of the year is Ullambana (Obon). The festival service for the Assembly at Ullambana (U-ram-bon-e) is held on July or August 14 and 15. This is a ceremony tracing itself back through China to ancient India; it is probably pre-Buddhist, but marks also the end of the Summer Rain Retreat of the clergy.

On December 31 many temples hold the Assembly for the Night of Ending (Jo-ya-e). At this New Year's Eve service the great bell is rung 108 times to mark the passing of the year.

Though not a special Shin holy day, the Festival of Flowers (Hana-matsuri) is observed in many Japanese temples and most Shin temples in the United States. The Nirvana Assembly (Nehan-e), called also Nirvana Day, and the Assembly for the Attainment of the Way (Jo-do-e) which is called Bodhi Day in English, are not always observed in Shin temples in Japan.

Official Buddhist Holidays observed in the Buddhist Churches of America circles are: (From "The Buddhist Holidays" published by Bureau of Buddhist Education)

January 1-New Year's Day (Shusho E)
This is a day of dedication. With renewed resolution we dedicate ourselves to the way of the Nembutsu.

January 16-Shinran Shonin Memorial Day (Ho-on-ko)
Ho-on-ko, meaning a gathering to express our gratitude, is a service in memory of Shinran Shonin (May 21, 1173-January 16, 1262) the founder of Jodo Shin Shu (True Pure Land Sect). Shinran Shonin was the first to teach absolute faith in Amida Buddha.

February 15-Nirvana Day (Nehan E)
On this day we solemnly observe the passing of Sakyamuni into Nirvana. Although he attained enlightenment and became a Bud-

71

dha, he was still in his earthly form. This earthly form, subject to birth and death, had to perish but his Teaching embodying the spirit of Buddhahood is eternal.

March 21-Higan (Higan E)

Higan, meaning Other Shore, is a service conducted during the spring equinox. At this time the weather is neither too warm nor too cold; the days and nights are of equal length. Harmony pervades throughout the universe. Therefore, we gather before the sacred shrine of Amida Buddha and meditate on the harmony of nature and devote ourselves to the realization of this harmony in our inner lives.

April 8-Buddha Day (Hanamatsuri)

This service is held to commemorate the birth of Gautama in Lumbini Garden. Amida, the Buddha of Infinite Wisdom and Compassion, manifested Himself among men in the person Gautama.

During the service a flower shrine known as Hanamido is set up in front of the main shrine as a symbol of Lumbini Garden. In this shrine is placed a statuette of the infant Buddha and the congregation offer flowers and pour sweet tea over the image. According to the ancient legend, the universe was filled with joyful music, flowers bloomed in full glory and sweet rain fell from the heavens to make this a joyful event.

May 21-Shinran Shonin Day (Shuso Gotan E)

Shinran Shonin was born near Kyoto on May 21, 1173. The loss of both parents at an early age moved him to enter the Buddhist priesthood. He studied for 20 years on Mt. Hiei, the site of 3000 monasteries where he endured the most difficult of meditations and practices.

At the age of 29 he abandoned the method of finding enlightenment by his self power (jiriki) and placed his faith in Amida's power (tariki) to realize Buddhahood.

July 15-Bon

An ancient legend tells us that during the time of the Buddha, one of the disciples, Moggallana, saw with his superhuman sight the agony of his mother as she suffered in the lowest hell. When this fact was brought to the attention of the Blessed One, his heart was moved to great compassion. Through the grace of his all embracing compassion the woman was saved. Moggallana and the other disciples clapped their hands in joy. The legend says this was the origin of the Bon odori. Bon, therefore, being an occasion for rejoicing in the enlightenment offered by the Buddha, is often referred to as a "Gathering of Joy."

September 1-BCA Founding Day (Beikoku Bukkyo Kaikyo Kinenbi)

The Reverend Shuye Sonoda and the Reverend Kakuryo Nishijima, dispatched by the Nishi Honganji to minister to the Buddhists in America, arrived in San Francisco on September 1, 1899. This day marks the official introduction of Jodo Shin Shu into the mainland United States.

Thus, September 1 has been designated as BCA Founding Day by the Buddhist Churches of America. It is observed with appropriate services and activities.

September 23-Higan (Higan E)

It has been a long Buddhist tradition to gather in our temples twice a year during the spring and autumnal equinox to recall the Six Perfections-Giving, Behaviour, Endurance, Endeavour, Meditation and Wisdom-and humbly put them into practice.

December 8-Bodhi Day (Jodo E)

Gautama meditated under the Bodhi Tree (Tree of Enlightenment and became a Buddha, perfect in Wisdom and Compassion. This historic event took place on December 8 as the first faint light of day began to glow in the eastern sky. By his example he showed us that it was possible for man to become a Buddha-a fully Enlightened Person. We are, therefore, in possession of this potentiality—Buddha-Nature—which, when awakened and cultivated, will enable us to achieve supreme Wisdom and Compassion.

December 31-New Year's Eve (Joya E)

On New Year's Eve we meditate on the countless blessings we have received throughout the year and express our gratitude to our parents, our nation, all beings and Amida Buddha.

Questions (to be answered in writing)

1. What does the word feast day mean? 2. Do all Buddhists celebrate the same holy days? 3. What services must every Shin temple have? 4. When are memorial services for Shinran held each month? 5. What other memorial services are held almost monthly? 6. What is the first holy day of the Year? 7. When is it held? 8. What is the purpose of the Assembly of the First Day? 9. How many days is the Proper Memorial celebrated? 10. When is the Feast of Thanksgiving and Gratitude? 11. What is the purpose of the Feast of Thanksgiving and Gratitude? 12. When is the Assembly for the Great Master Enko held? 13. Who is Enko? 14. What feastday is celebrated in March and in September? 15. What does equinox mean? 16. Why are the night and day equal? (Check an encyclopedia) 17. Where did the Equinoctal Assembly originate? 18. About when did the Equinoctal Assembly originate? 19. What does C.E. mean? 20. When is Shinran's birthday celebrated? 21. What names are used for the feast day marking Shinran's birthday? 22. Who was Shotoku? 23. What feast day celebrates the memory of Shotoku? 24. When is the feast day which commemorates Shotoku? 25. On what day do we mark the foundation of the Shin sect? 26. What is the name of the feast day which commemorates the founding of the Shin sect? 27. When is Ullambana celebrated? 28. What is the purpose of Ullambana? 29. What is the last important service of the year? 30. What is the Festival of Flowers called in Japanese? 31. What two holy days are often not celebrated in Shin Temples in Japan?

HANAMATSURI AND OBON

American Buddhists who have received their religion from the temples of China, Korea, or Japan celebrate two important festivals each year. Because some Buddhists use a sun calendar and others use a moon calendar, they do not all celebrate these festivals on the very same day.

The first of these holy days is in the spring, on the eighth day of the fourth month. This is sometimes called the Festival of Flowers (Hanamatsuri), and it commemorates the birth of Sakyamuni Buddha in India. Some people call this festival Wesak. However, Wesak is actually a different festival. Wesak celebrates on one day the Birth, Englightenment, and Death of Sakyamuni. This is the practice of Buddhists in South Asia, and it is quite a different festival from Hanamatsuri, which celebrates only the birth of Sakyamuni.

The second of these two great holy days comes at the end of summer, on the fifteenth day of the seventh month. In ancient times, this marked the end of the summer retreat of the monks. During the rainy summer Buddhist monks retreated to the monastery, and did not go out until the end of the rainy season. When the rains were over, they could again visit the houses of the ordinary lay Buddhists. The laymen then gave them new robes and other proper gifts, and there was great joy that the monks would come again to teach Buddhism.

There is a legend that one year at this time, Elder Mogallana saw a vision of his mother in hell. He asked Sakyamuni Buddha how she might be freed from her suffering. Sakyamuni said all sentient beings are freed from suffering by hearing the Law. Mogallana preached a sermon. By the merit of his preaching, his mother was freed from suffering. Then, it is said, everyone danced for joy. So it is that Buddhists dance at this festival which is called Obon. Actually, this legend is later than the practice of celebrating the festival, and it is only a parable to teach us a lesson.

It is said that Mogallana's mother was suffering in hell. She was hanging upside down. To Buddhists, our heaven and our hell is in our own minds. We are all in hell when our thinking and our doing make us suffer. When we are not upright and happy, we are upside-down in a hell of our own making.

The practice of the festival of Obon is much older than this parable. It is a time when we remember the dead and our debt to them. We know that we can best repay this debt by hearing the teachings of Buddha and visiting our temples.

In the *Sutra of the Observation after the Death of the Buddha* we read that Sakyamuni was once in a park called the Jetavana. This park was near the city of Sravasti in India. Sakyamuni was preaching to a great crowd. Ananda, his favorite disciple, stepped out of the crowd, bowed, and spoke to the Buddha.

"How," asked Ananda, "are the followers of Buddha to celebrate days after the death of Sakyamuni?"

The Buddha answered Ananda and told him what ought to be done on the eighth day of the fourth month, and on the fifteenth day of the seventh month.

"On these days," the Buddha said, "to save mankind whom they wish to be happy, everyone should share their money and treasures. People should share the rare things which they prize. They can then be put to use for the welfare of the world. People should also give lights and incense to the temples for use in making sutras and statues.

"Offer food to the monks and give charity to the poor. Arrange for a memorial assembly (in the temple), or you cannot receive donations. If, afterwards, you do not distribute these donations, this is the sin of destroying the Buddha in this very world."

This is the real meaning of our holy days; they are an opportunity for us to be generous. We take this occasion to express our thanksgiving and gratitude to all sentient beings. We know that our happiness is dependent upon every sentient being in the universe. On our holy days we especially think of this, and we give thanks for the happiness we have had in our religion.

On these days, too, we know we must share our happiness with the sick, the poor, and the oppressed. We realize also that we can only show our gratitude by handing on our religion to future generations.

We share what we have, whether it be money, our services, our time, or our happiness. We give to the poor, the lonely, the weak, and the aged. We give to our temples which in turn share these donations with those who are in need. We give to the Buddha who is ever present in the truth of his teaching.

The way we celebrate these festivals is to remind us of the wonderful teachings of our religion. The flowers at Hanamatsuri remind us of Lumbini. The sweet tea we pour over the image of the child Buddha on that day reminds us of the gentle rains which fell to bathe the child. The dancing of the Obon festival reminds us of the joy and happiness of hearing the Law of Buddha.

But these holy days are not just to remind us of the past. They are a chance for the scout to put his thanksgiving into action. These holy days are a chance to look ahead. The scout should try to pass on his religion to the future, and he can do this by celebrating these two holy days in the way Buddha taught.

Questions (to be answered in writing)

1. Why are these two important festivals celebrated on different days by different people? 2. On what day of what months is the first of the two holy days celebrated? 3. What is it called in English? 4. What is it called in Japanese? 5. What does the Festival of Flowers commemorate? 6. Is Hanamatsuri the same as Wesak? 7. How do Wesak and Hanamatsuri differ? 8. What is the date of the second of the two important holy days? 9. What did this date mark in ancient times? 10. What does the word retreat mean? 11. What did the monks do during the rainy season? 12. Why were the laymen happy when the rainy season was over? 13. Where was Mogallana's mother? 14. What did Mogallana ask the Buddha? 15. What did the Buddha tell Mogallana to do? 16. Why did everyone dance for joy? 17. When are we upside-down in hell? 18. How did the Buddha say these two festivals were to be celebrated? 19. What do we express on these two holy days? 20. What do we share on these days? 21. To whom do we give on these days? 22. What does the tea poured over the Buddha remind us of? 23. What do the flowers of Hanamatsuri remind us of? 24. What is the dancing at Obon to remind us of?

THE WISTERIA CREST

In Japan the use of family and temple crests is not yet a thousand years old, and it is less than five hundred years ago that they became very popular. One of the best known crests is the Chrysanthemum Crest of the Japanese Imperial family.

The Hino family, of which Shinran was a son, had a Heron (tsuru) Crest. The Ohtani family at Nishi Honganji still use this crest on many of its utensils. This Heron Crest, then, is the family crest of Shinran.

The Honganji, however, uses today a double Wisteria Crest. But it has used this only for the last eighty or ninety years. In olden days, the Honganji used the Imperial Crest!

In the sixteenth century, the Emperor gave Nishi Honganji the special right to use the Imperial family crest. For several hundred years, down until about 1870, the Honganji used this crest as a symbol on many utensils, and even today most of the antiques bearing this crest which are sold come from the Honganji originally. But in modern times, a law was passed which forbid any but the Imperial family to use this crest.

When this law was passed, the Honganji had to find a new temple crest. At this time the famous Kujo family of the Fujiwara clan offered its family crest to the Honganji for its use. So it is that the Wisteria Crest is the family crest of the Kujo family. It is a symbol which has a long and important history in the orient, and in Japan. Wisteria itself originated perhaps in India, or in Southern China; but the plant plays no important part in the traditional symbolism of these countries.

The wisteria flower indicates, in Japanese tradition, humility and a cordial welcome. Thus it is particularly fitting to symbolize the Honganji which welcomes to its fellowship people of all races. Wisteria blossoms are symbolic of brightness and transitoriness.

Therefore, though the Wisteria Crest has no ancient history in its connection with the Honganji, it still is representative of all the essentials of the Buddhist religion.

Questions (to be answered in writing)

1. What was the crest of Shinran's family? 2. What was the family name of Shinran? 3. What is now the crest of the Honganji? 4. What was formerly the Honganji crest? 5. Why was the Honganji obliged to stop using the Chrysanthemum Crest? 6. Where did the Honganji get its new crest? 7. Who is the Kujo family? 8. Is wisteria important in the symbolism of India and China? 9. What does the wisteria indicate in Japanese tradition? 10. Why is it fitting that a flower symbolizing welcome be the crest of the Honganji? 11. Of what is wisteria symbolic?

THE LOTUS

The flower of the lotus is the great symbol of Buddhism. The Buddha often spoke of the lotus. The lotus grows with its roots in slime and filth. Its stem rises up through the dirty water, and its bud appears above the water. The lotus blooms, then, white and pure above the level of the dirty water. The Buddha said his followers should be like this. Though Buddhists live in a world filled with the filth of evil, they should rise above it. Speaking of the good and pure people who rejoice in the Teachings, the *Shoshinge* quotes the Buddha: "These people are called the pundarika (white lotus)." Buddhists should raise themselves towards Enlightenment. They should rise from the slimy and dirty world about them. They should bloom forth pure and beautiful above the common level. They should make themselves spiritually beautiful, so others, too, can enjoy the truth.

Thus, the lotus is the symbol of the path of Buddhism. Nothing symbolizes better the goal of our religion.

Questions (to be answered in writing)

1. Where does the lotus have its roots? 2. Where does the flower bloom? 3. Why does the Buddha liken his followers to the lotus? 4. What is the most perfect symbol of the Buddhist religion?

SYMBOLIC ANIMALS

In many Buddhist buildings and monuments we see animals used as symbols. The elephant and the lion are most common. But we see also the bull, the horse, the crane, the turtle and the deer, and others.

The elephant, of course, symbolizes the conception of the Buddha, because his mother dreamed of an elephant before he was born. The elephant also brings to mind a sense of calmness and dignity. His calm and careful walk reminds us of the mind and actions of the saint. The bull represents the birth of the Buddha, for Sakyamuni was born under the astrological sign of Taurus (the bull). The lion symbolizes the first sermon; for the Buddha preaches with the loud, clear, authoritative voice of a lion. The horse represents the renunciation of the prince, when his horse died of a broken heart.

The deer is sometimes used as a symbol of the first sermon, for it was preached in the deer park at Benares. Also, because of stories when the bodhisattva lived as a deer, this animal also represents self-sacrifice. For, as king of the deer, the bodhisattva sacrificed his own life to save the lives of his followers.

The crane and the turtle are symbols of long life. Because of this, they have come to represent endless life in the Pure Realm of Nirvana. The story of the turtle winning the race is one of the famous Buddhist parables, so the turtle also symbolizes slow but steady progress in religion.

Questions (to be answered in writing)

1. What does the turtle symbolize? 2. What does the elephant represent as a symbol? 3. What do the crane and the turtle represent? 4. What is represented by the symbol of the bull? 5. What is symbolized by the lion? 6. What is the symbol of the horse to bring to mind? 7. What is represented by the symbol of the deer? 8. What is a symbol? (Check your dictionary or encyclopedia).

THE WHEEL

One of the most frequent symbols found in Buddhist art is the wheel. It is pictured in many forms. It is sometimes called the Wheel of the Law or the Wheel of Life. "Turning the Wheel of the Law" means preaching the doctrine of the Buddha.

The eight spokes of the wheel represent the Noble Eight-fold Path. Their equal length symbolizes justice. The tire around the wheel represents the all-embracing Wisdom of Buddhahood. The hub reminds us of modesty and thoughtfulness. The axle is the bar of Truth upon which the Wheel turns. The actual revolving of the Wheel symbolizes the round of rebirth. Rebirth, sometimes wrongly called reincarnation, binds us to life.

The Wheel, then, reminds us of most of the great truths of Buddhist doctrine.

Questions (to be answered in writing)

1. What is the symbolic of the wheel called? 2. What is meant by "turning the wheel"? 3. What do the spokes represent? 4. What represents justice? 5. What does the tire of the wheel represent? 6. What does the hub symbolize? 7. What does the axle bar represent? 8. What symbolizes rebirth?

THE OBJECT OF REVERENCE

On the altar in our temples there usually is the image of the Buddha Amida. It is a standing image covered with gold. The image has the thumb and forefinger of each hand touching; they form a circle. The circle represents perfection, without beginning or end. The image's left hand stretches down in compassion to every suffering being in all the worlds. The right hand, raised in wisdom, depicts the search for Nirvana. For both the wisdom and the compassion of Buddhahood are perfect and complete. The Buddha is shown with one foot forward. This symbolizes his stepping down to help and to teach mankind.

Amida Buddha is that aspect of Buddhahood which is infinite light and infinite life. If we think of Buddha in terms of space, he is infinite light; if we consider Buddha with regard to time, he is infinite life. Abiding in spaceless, timeless Enlightenment, Amida is not merely a Buddha, but the very essence of Buddhahood itself.

The Amida image represents also the virtues of self-enlightenment and enlightening others, which we see in the career of Sakyamuni. Thus, in Shin Buddhism, Sakyamuni and Amida are not separate Buddhas; they are one and the same. They are different only as far as they are differing aspects of the same Perfect and Complete Enlightenment.

The image of the Buddha is made according to ancient tradition. This tradition lists thirty-two marks or signs of the Buddha. The seventeenth mark is a golden colored skin. The fifth mark is blue eyes. The second mark is wooly or kinky hair. These marks suggest the racial heritage of the Buddha.

Sakyamuni was born in northeast India. This was an area where the Mongolian peoples of northern Asia mingled with the Negroid natives and the Caucasian invader. From the Mongolians Shakyamuni derived his beautiful golden skin. From the Caucasian Ariyans, he inherited the blue eyes. And from negroid ancestors he inherited his hair, which even on ordinary images is noticeable. The Buddha, thus, is a unity of what is best in all races, just as he is a unity of the best of all truths.

In our home, Shin sectators usually do not use a statue of the Buddha. We use a painted scroll in our family shrines, or, more often, we use a scroll with the Name and Title of the Buddha written on it in Chinese. The name and title is the phrase: Namu Amida Butsu.

Some people might mistake the image of the Buddha for an idol. So we use a picture. But, even a picture does not show us the real Buddha. The real, true Buddha is present only in his Name and Title, so we use the scroll with the words Namu Amida

Buddha. This, we think, is the best representation of the Buddha.

Whichever representation we use, it has only one purpose. We do not worship the image or the picture of the Buddha. They are only aids to our thinking. The peace and calm we see in the Buddha's image reminds us that we too should strive toward Buddhahood.

Questions (to be answered in writing)

1. What is the position of each hand on the Buddha image? 2. What is represented by the two fingers of each hand which form a circle? 3. What does the forward foot of the image represent? 4. What is Amida? 5. What two aspects of Sakyamuni's career do we see in the image? 6. What does aspects mean? 7. How are Amida and Sakyamuni the same or different? 8. How many marks are found in picturing the Buddha? 9. What racial heritage do the marks of the Buddha suggest? 10. What three forms of representation of the Buddha are found in shrines? 11. Which is most common to Shin homes? 12. What is the Name and Title of Buddha? 13. What is the purpose of a Buddha image?

ETIQUETTE

The forms of religious etiquette are frequently belittled as unimportant. Such views arise from a misunderstanding of the purpose and foundation of etiquette.

Indian Yoga, from its earliest times and in all its many forms has insisted that form is of utmost importance in spiritual development, and the Buddha Sakyamuni laid down minute details of proper etiquette for cleric and layman.

In modern times, as well, we have seen the importance placed upon form by the military of various nations, by sportsmen and by artists.

The outward form with which a thing is accomplished is

closely related to the inner spirit with which it is undertaken. Thus Buddhism teaches that form and content cannot be separated any more than redness can be separated from the rose.

Buddhists never run nor shout in temple, and boy scouts, especially need to be careful about this. Often they are using the temple building at the same time as other groups. Boy scouts then should be very careful not to make unnecessary noises which will disturb other people in the temple. Many buildings are used for various purposes at the same time, and the chapel is frequently part of the same building that must be used for all other activities. Scouts should keep this in mind.

When one appears before the Buddha carrying himself with dignity and solemnity, the heart shares in the spirit of worship and reverence. When the heart is reverent and sincere, one naturally bears himself with that solemn dignity which is the foundation of all etiquette.

In a Japanese style temple, one seats himself with his back straight. The trunk is held upright, the knees about three inches apart (women place their knees together). The eyes look to a place about ten feet before one. The hand's palms down, are placed naturally on the lap, with the left hand folded above the other.

One stands with ones heels together. Men open their feet at an angle of thirty degrees, while women keep their feet together. The body is to be held upright and straight. One stands naturally, looking to a point about thirty feet ahead.

In sitting upon a chair or in a pew, one should sit upright, with the toes together, the knees about three inches apart (but women place their knees together), the eyes looking to a point about fifteen feet in front of the person. The hands are placed in the same way as when one sits Japanese style.

In all cases, the rosary or beads is held in the left hand.

Questions (to be answered in writing)
    1. According to Confucianism what three things are in-

volved in proper etiquette? 2. Name some modern activities where form is very important. 3. Should one run or shout in the temple? 4. What is the natural foundation of all etiquette? 5. How should one sit in a temple where the seating is in Japanese style? 6. How does one stand in a temple? 7. How does one sit in a temple pew? 8. In what hand is the rosary to be held?

BEADS

The beads (o-juzu) or rosary are an important object in Buddhist life. Rennyo of the Honganji said that to go before the Buddha without beads is like grabbing the Buddha in one's bare hands. It is, Rennyo said, rude not to use beads in the temple.

In India chaplets of beads were originally made of various kinds of seeds. They were put on a string. They were used as counters to remember things, and they were called remembrancers. Sometimes they were used to count the number of times the Three Treasures were recited. Sometimes they were used to remember other important doctrines.

A full set of Buddhist beads usually has 108 beads, but half sets of 54, and quarter sets of 27 are used. There are many explanations of the meaning of the beads. This is natural, because the beads were used by different people to remember different things.

The 108 beads recall the 108 human passions for some people; for other people these 108 beads recall the 108 Brahmans who foretold Sakyamuni's future when he was born. Some people use the half chaplet to recall the 54 steps in a Bodhisattva's career. The chaplet of 27 beads is sometimes said to represent the 27 ranks of the saints, Shinram mentions these ranks in the *Teaching, Practice, Faith and Attainment.* Small chaplets do not always have a set number of beads. Often the maker puts in enough beads to make it look balanced when worn.

Some Shin teachers say that the three larger beads are

symbolic of the Three Teasures: Buddha, Dharma, Sangha. There are, of course, many other explanations, and different sects will give different names to each bead and assign different meanings to them. This is only to be expected. For the beads are used to recall what their owner wants to remember. They have meaning, only if you give each bead a meaning!

In some sects the beads are counted even today, and in many sects they are rubbed together between the palms. In Shin, however, they are never counted and they are never rubbed together. Sometimes they are passed through the fingers, though even this is mostly a custom of former ages.

In Shin today the beads are just put over the two hands with their palms put together. The Honganji branch lets the tassle fall naturally to the bottom. This putting of the beads over the hands holds them together tightly. This symbolizes the doctrine of Buddha and Ordinary Man being of One Essence (butsu-bon-it-tai).

Buddhist beads are never to be laid where people sit or walk. The beads are never carried into a toilet or such places.

Questions (to be answered in writing)

1. What is the Japanese word for beads? 2. What did Rennyo say of going before a shrine without beads. 3. Of what were chaplets originally made? 4. What is the meaning of the word chaplet? 5. For what were chaplets originally used? 6. What name was applied to beads because they are used to recall things? 7. What was often recited with the beads? 8. How many beads are there in a full set. 9. What does the full chaplet of 108 beads recall? 10. What might the half chaplet recall? 11. What might the quarter chaplet recall from Shinran's writings? 12. Why do small chaplets often have irregular numbers of beads? 13. What meaning do some people give to the three larger beads? 14. Are there other explanations? 15. Does Shin use the beads for counting? 16. How does Shin use the beads today? 17. What does the

chaplet symbolize when it holds the two hands together? 18. Where should beads never be put?

THE CANDLES ON THE ALTAR

The candles on the altar are, of course, for light. But they are of greater significance, for light is symbolic of Amida Buddha, of Enlightenment, of Truth, of Goodness, and much more. Candles also are often used in similes in Buddhist scriptures, and King Milinda was taught about life by a monk who likened it to a candle-flame.

The candle flame gives us a continuous light, but each second the flame is new. Each flame gives birth to the next tongue of flame. If you take a candle flame and light a new candle, nothing passes from one flame to the other. In the same way life continues through eternity, with nothing passing from one life to another. Each second of life is a new creation, and it only appears to be continuous. Right now, we are dying and being born many times each second. Even at the death of our bodies life flows on like the flame of the candle passing from one candle to another.

On the altar Buddhists use dripless bees-wax candles if the traditional Japanese or Chinese candles are not available. Most candles in the Orient from ancient times are made of vegetable tallow. In Japan and China they are made from the seeds of certain trees. Candles made of animal tallow should not be used on the altar.

The Japanese candles are made by hand, and layer after layer of tallow is rolled onto the candle. The top and bottom of the candle are larger in circumference than the middle, so that its shape might be called concave. The wick is uniformly paper. These candles are usually not available in the United States. Here we often use any good quality candle instead. But we try to use candles of the traditional colors. For ordinary use the outside of the candles is traditionally red, but white candles are used on special occasions.

In Shin temples, gold colored candles are used for happy ceremonies; silver, for funerals; white, for funerals (when silver is unavailable); and for the services during the forty-nine days of mourning, and at the memorial services in the first and third year after a death. At all other times, Shin uses red candles.

In the Buddhist Churches of America temples white candles are generally used. Red candles are used only during special holidays.

Questions (to be answered in writing)

1. What is the chief purpose of the candles on the altar? 2. What do the candles and their light symbolize? 3. How does candle-flame remind one of life? 4. What kind of Western-style candles should be used on the altar? 5. What kind of tallow is used for candles in the Orient? 6. What shape do Japanese altar candles have? 7. What color candles should ordinarily be used in Shin services in U.S.?

FLOWERS ON THE ALTAR

At the time of the Buddha, animal sacrifices were common in India's religions. But the Buddha disapproved of killing. So Buddhists did not sacrifice animals in their religious services. Instead, the Buddhists make offerings of fresh flowers. These were placed upon the altar in vases, or sometimes trays were brought which were heaped high with blossoms. In some temples even today, the blossom alone is used, without any stem.

Flowers are among the most beautiful things in the world. Yet, they are impermanent. They are transient. When they are most beautiful, the softest wind can destroy them. The odor of the flowers pleases us. Their shapes and colors give us pleasure. But, in a moment they are gone.

In the life of flowers is death. In their growth there is

decay. Even in their beauty is their destruction. They symbolize for us the nature of suffering and sorrow. They symbolize the round of life, for as the flower forms the seeds for rebirth, our own thoughts and acts form the causes of our own rebirth.

We usually have also evergreen branches on our altars. Many different evergreen trees and bushes are used. Usually they have seedpods on the branches. These symbolize the eternal nature of Nirvana, and the seeds represent the completion of the goal.

From the use of flowers on the altar, the art of flower arrangement arose. In Japan and China arranging flowers is an important aspect of culture, and men and women take lessons for years. From this activity, they learn some of the truths of Buddhism.

Questions (to be answered in writing)
1. What did Buddhists substitute for animal sacrifice in religion? 2. How do flowers symbolize suffering? 3. What do evergreen branches symbolize? 4. What is represented by the seedpods on the evergreen branches?

INCENSE

In our temple services we use incense. We see the solid incense, then we see its smoke. Then, after the smoke disappears, we still can smell the incense in the farthest corner of the temple.

The incense is useless unless it is used; then it makes pleasant the farthest nook of the temple. So, too, are man's deeds. Evil deeds, though they seem to disappear, still affect the whole world about us. But good deeds, though they are not seen, perfume our world. A spoken word or an action, like the incense, reaches far out into the community. So we burn incense to remind ourselves that we, too, are like the incense. We are useless until we act, and our acts influence many people that we do not know, for our acts reach out into the farthest corner of the community.

Often we burn our incense in special burners. These sometimes have fancy lids, decorated with lions or dragons. But these burners have no special meaning, and the animals symbolize nothing; they are merely convenient to use as handles.

Questions (to be answered in writing)

1. How does incense symbolize the actions of our lives? 2. What is the symbolic significance of the lion or the dragon on the top of the incense burner?

GONGS, BELLS AND DRUMS

In Buddhists services gongs, bells and drums are used. At New Years, for example, the great temple bells are rung one hundred and eight times. These remind us of the passions and the virtues which make up human life. Some of the gongs are used only to punctuate the reading of the scriptures; that is, they ring to call attention to important sentences. Some gongs or bells tell people when to join in the chanting. Also, some gongs are beat to start the procession of ministers at a very large ceremony. At many temples the great bell or the drum is beat to call people to the services.

But all the gongs, bells and drums have another importance. Their various sounds are symbolic. These sounds are impermanent. You can hear them rise and fall. You can hear them fade and die away. These sounds, then, remind us of the impermanence of the ego. They remind us that we, too, are impermanent.

Questions (to be answered in writing)

1. What are four ways in which the gongs, bells and drums are used for a very practical reason? 2. What is the symbolic significance of the instruments in the temple?

THE BUDDHIST IN SOCIETY

It is a difficult thing to be a Buddhist in a country that has few Buddhists. Some people do not think so. They say Buddhism has always gotten along in every country. They say Buddhism has always changed to fit a new country. Such people say we should change Buddhism to fit a new time and a new place. These people are ready to give up anything. They just want to get along with everybody. They even fear to say they are Buddhists.

But real Buddhists will not give up everything just to get along. True Buddhists know their religion is a great treasure. They will not give up important parts of their religion. They are not afraid to say they are Buddhists. Yet, they are not always shouting that they follow the Buddha's teaching.

To Buddhists, religion is a private affair. We are not to force our religion upon others. We are not to argue with people who want to force their religion upon us. Rennyo of the Honganji has said: "Now if there is a person who, having heard the substance of the awakening of faith by the Other Power (ta-riki) within this stream, has fixed and determined it, and, according to his awakening of faith, sets it at the bottom of his heart, he shall not discuss it in comparison with other teachings and other people. Moreover, he is not, in the lanes and highways and even in the places of his dwelling, to utter its praises openly and without concern." (Epistles 2:6). These ideas are to lead the Buddhist, and it is important that we understand their true meaning.

Rennyo does not, of course, mean we should never talk about Buddhism with people. He means we must not force our views upon others. We should invite people to visit our temples; we should answer questions that are asked in full sincerity. Nonetheless, we should never be embarrased to say that we cannot easily explain Buddhism; yet this answer can be used as an opportunity to invite a person to our services.

But in our every-day life we are often asked questions about religion. "What church do you go to . . .?" and a hundred other questions confront us daily. Our religion urges us to reply,

"Oh, that really isn't important." "I'd really rather not discuss religion." "It is quite unprofitable to talk about religion."

As to questions on questionnaires, it is not deceitful nor improper to ignore them. At school or any public institution, the government has the right to inquire into your religion. Rennyo has said that the Shin sectator (follower) "is to be more and more exacting in public affairs." A Christian missionary, William Elliot Griffis, has defined Shin social characteristics in a way which shows how Shin has applied these words of Rennyo to life: "Liberty of thought and action, and incoercible desire to be free of governmental, traditional, ultra-ecclesiastical or Shinto influence ... is characteristic of the great sect founded by Shinran ... " *(The Religions of Japan,* New York, 1896, p. 274.) The spirit of Shin in cases where government forms ask after religion is to ignore the question or quietly decline to answer it.

In cases of public oaths such as in courts, Federal and State laws provide at every occasion for an alternate oath. This alternate oath does not include words such as "So help me God." A person has merely to say: "An oath calling on God does not conform with the teachings of my religion; may I have an alternate form of affirmation." Courts administer such alternate forms every day to Quakers, secularists, and other persons who request them.

Perhaps for ordinary American Buddhists, the greatest problem arises with the salute to the flag. The words of this pledge were composed by a Christian minister who carefully did not mention God. However, in recent years the words under God were added to the pledge. This immediately created a serious problem for Buddhists. Our religion does not include a belief in God. The courts, however, have declared that these words may be omitted from the pledge, and Buddhists should feel free to do so. In reciting the pledge in public with others, they can easily remain silent while those two words are spoken. In Buddhist meetings, the original pledge without this recent addition should be used. In a large meeting, a prepared slide can be flashed on a screen. The master of ceremonies can quietly say: "We invite you now to renew your allegiance to our flag by reciting together the Pledge of Allegiance as it is on the screen.

Being a Buddhist in a non-Buddhist or even a Buddhist country is not an easy goal at any time. It means that each individual Buddhist must accept full responsibility for his own practice of the path of Bodhisattva. This path is a way of life which seeks to help all people to be fully and completely free. To reach this, the individual Buddhist must make his own decisions as to what will best advance the cause of freedom in the world.

However, in any country the Buddhist can quietly and calmly insist upon his rights. By this, he extends the freedom and rights of all that country's citizens. When Quakers or Unitarians have secured, through the Supreme Court, their own rights to refuse to serve as combat soldiers, they have extended the rights of all Americans towards greater freedom; when Jehovah's Witnesses, in the Supreme Court, won their right to preach their religion on the public street or from door to door, they extended the rights of all Americans to greater freedom of speech.

When a Buddhist makes use of an alternate oath in court, he keeps alive the custom and extends its right to every citizen. When he refuses to declare his religion, the Buddhist protects the privacy of religious opinion for all citizens. This, on the social level, is part of what the bodhisattva truly means when he vows never to accept freedom unless it is available to all sentient beings: his exercise of freedom creates the freedom of all beings.

Questions (to be answered in writing)

1. Is it proper for Buddhists to argue about religion with people of other faiths? 2. What does Rennyo mean when he says of Buddhism: " ... The Buddhist is not to utter Buddhism's praises openly and without concern"? 3. What can we say to people who ask what religion we follow? 4. Should we never tell people what religion we believe? 5. What is the Shin attitude toward government interest in religion? 6. In court, do Buddhists

have to swear by "Almighty God"? 7. What kind of oath may Buddhists take in courts? 8. Do Buddhists have to say "under God" when they say the flag salute? 9. How can Buddhists help make freedom strong for all people?

THE FUNDAMENTALS OF BUDDHISM; A SUMMARY

The truths upon which Buddhism is founded are natural. They are not mysterious revelations of any god. These truths are discovered and taught to the world by certain wise and merciful beings called Buddhas. The title Buddha means "Awakened" or "Enlightened." In different kalpas (world-periods) these truths have been discovered and taught by the Buddhas.

The last teacher in the present kalpa was Gautama Buddha, the Sage of the Sakyas. He was born in a royal family in India about 2500 years ago. Sakyamuni is a historical person, and his given name was Siddhartha.

Sakyamuni taught that ignorance produces desire; unsatisfied desire is the cause of rebirth; and rebirth is the cause of sorrow. To free oneself from sorrow, therefore, it is necessary to escape rebirth. To escape rebirth, it is necessary to get rid of desire; and to destroy desire, it is necessary to destroy ignorance.

Ignorance fosters the belief that rebirth is a necessary thing. When ignorance is destroyed, the worthlessness of every such rebirth, considered as an end in itself, is seen; and one awakes to the need of adopting a course of life by which the necessity of such repeated rebirths can be done away with. Ignorance also produces on one hand the false and illogical idea that there is only one existence for man; and on the other, ignorance produces the illusion that this one life is followed by states of unchangeable pleasure in a heaven or endless torment in a hell.

The end of all ignorance can be attained by the perservering practice of an all-embracing selflessness in conduct, development of intelligence, wisdom in thought, and destruction of desire for base personal pleasures.

The desire for existence is the cause of rebirth. When desire is extinguished, rebirths cease, and the perfected individual attains to that highest state of peace, understanding, and compassion. This state is called Nirvana.

Sakyamuni taught that ignorance can be dispelled and sorrow removed by the knowledge of the Four Noble Truths. These are (1) the sufferings of existence; (2) the cause which produces suffering, this is the ever-renewed desire to satisfy one's self, for this end can never be attained; and (3) the destruction of such desire, or the removal of oneself from it—the means of obtaining this destruction of desire. He taught the means of this destruction to be the Noble Eightfold path: (1) Right Views, (2) Right Mindedness, (3) Right Speech, (4) Right Action, (5) Right Livelihood, (6) Right Endeavor, (7) Right Mindfulness, and (8) Right Concentration.

Right Concentration leads to spiritual enlightenment, or the development of that Buddha potentiality which is in every man.

The essence of Buddhism is summed up by Buddha himself in a verse in the Dhammapada:

> To cease from all evil,
> To do good,
> To purify one's own heart:
> This is the teaching of the Buddhas.

Buddhists are taught to show the same tolerance, forbearance, and brotherly love to all men, without distinction, and an unswerving kindness towards the members of the animal and plant kingdoms.

The universe was evolved, not created. It functions according to law, not according to the caprice of any god.

The universe is subject to a natural causation known as karma. The merits and demerits of a being in past existences determine his condition in the present one. Each man, therefore, has created the causes of the effects which he now experiences.

The obstacles to the attainment of good karma may be

removed by the observance of the five basic precepts which are part of the moral code of Buddhism: (1) Kill not; (2) Steal not; (3) Be not unchaste; (4) Lie not; (5) Abstain from harmful or stupefying drugs or liquors.

Buddhism discourages superstitious credulity. Gautama Buddha taught it to be the duty of a parent to have his child educated in science and literature. He taught also that no one should believe what is spoken by any sage, written in any book, or affirmed by any tradition, unless it accords with reason.

Questions (to be answered in writing)
1. Is Buddhism a revealed religion? 2. What does "Buddha" mean? 3. What does "kalpa" mean? 4. Where was Gautama Buddha born? 5. When was Gautama Buddha born? 6. What was the Buddha's given name? 7. What produces desire? 8. What is the cause of rebirth? 9. What is necessary to escape rebirth? 10. What produces the notion that there is an eternal heaven or an endless hell? 11. How can an end of ignorance be achieved? 12. To what state does the perfected being attain? 13. What are the Four Noble Truths? 14. What is the Noble Eightfold Path? 15. What verse sums up the Buddha's teaching? 16. What are Buddhists to show to all men? 17. How are Buddhists to treat animals? 18. Was the earth created or did it evolve? 19. What is the natural law of causation called? 20. What determines one's condition in life? 21. What are the Five Precepts? 22. Does Buddhism encourage superstition? 23. What measure should be used in listening, reading and action?

THE DREAM OF QUEEN MAYA

The land is India. The time is two thousand five hundred years and more ago. In the city of Kapilavasthu the midsummer festival was proclaimed, and all the people began to get ready to celebrate.

Queen Maya celebrated the festival with flowers and perfumes. On the seventh day she rose early, performed the holy-day vows, and then she entered again the royal bed-chamber.

Lying on the royal bed, she fell asleep and dreamed this dream: Four kings raised her together with her bed and took her to the Himalayas. Placing her beneath a great sal-tree, they stood to one side. Then their queens decked Queen Maya with divine flowers. Not far from there, she dreamed, is Silver Mountain, and on it is a golden palace. Here a bed was prepared for Queen Maya, and she lay upon it. A white elephant then climbed Silver Mountain, going to it from the north. In his trunk, like a silver chain, the white elephant carried a white lotus. He trumpeted, entered the golden palace, made a rightwise circle three times around the Queen's bed, and seemed to enter her body.

The next day, on awakening, Queen Maya told her dream to the King. King Suddhodana called many Brahman wise men and prepared splendid seats for them. He filled the gold and silver bowls of the Brahmans with cooked ghee, honey, sugar and excellent rice. Then he gave them many gifts. When they were delighted with all these pleasures, he told them the Queen's dream.

"What will take place?" asked the King.

The Brahman wise men said, "King Suddhodana, be not anxious. You will have a son. If he lives a household life, he will become a universal monarch. If he leaves his house and goes forth from the world to become a monk, he will become a Buddha. He will destroy the darkness and error of the world."

Questions (to be answered in writing)

1. In what land was the Buddha born? 2. About how long ago was the Buddha born? 3. What festival was proclaimed in Kapilavastu? 4. With what did Queen Maya celebrate the festival? 5. What did Queen Maya do on the seventh day of the festival? 6. Where did the four kings take Queen Maya in her dream? 7. What climbed Silver Mountain and entered the golden

palace? 8. What did the white elephant carry in his trunk? 9. What did the elephant do in Queen Maya's dream? 10. To whom did Queen Maya tell her dream? 11. Whom did King Suddhodana call together? 12. What did the King give the Brahmans? 13. What did the King ask the Brahmans? 14. What did the Brahmans tell King Suddhodana? 15. What would happen if the child led a household life? 16. What does the word monarch mean? 17. What would happen if the son of the King left the world? 18. What does a Buddha destroy? 19. What does "leave the world" mean?

THE BIRTH OF GOTAMA

Queen Maya, when her time had come, desired to go to her relatives' home. She said to the King: "Your Majesty, I wish to go to the city of my people."

"As you wish," replied King Suddhodana, and he caused the road from Kapilavasthu to be made smooth. It was decorated with flowers, flags and banners. Then Queen Maya was seated in a palanquin carried by a thousand courtiers, and she set forth with a great company.

Between the two cities was a pleasure grove of sal-trees, called the Lumbini garden. It belonged to the inhabitants of both cities, and was then in full flower. Among the branches and flowers were bees and flocks of birds singing with sweet sounds. The whole of Lumbini seemed like a heavenly grove, or like a banquet pavilion decorated for a mighty king.

When Queen Maya saw Lumbini, the desire arose in her heart of sporting therein. The courtiers with the Queen entered the sal-grove. She went to the foot of a great royal sal-tree, and desired to take hold of a branch. Then she was shaken by the pangs of birth, and the multitude put a curtain around her and retired. Taking hold of the sal-branch, she was delivered. At that moment, the four Great Brahmans came and received the child and set him before his mother.

"Rejoice, O Queen, a mighty son is born to thee!" they said.

And two showers of water descended from the sky upon the child and his mother.

Questions (to be answered in writing)

1. What did Queen Maya desire when her time was come? 2. What did the Queen say to King Suddhodana? 3. Was the Queen allowed to go? 4. What did the King do? 5. How was the highway decorated? 6. How did the Queen Maya travel? 7. What is a palanquin? 8. Where was Lumbini Garden? 9. To whom did Lumbini Garden belong? 10. What was Lumbini Garden like? 11. What did Queen Maya desire when she passed Lumbini Garden? 12. What did Queen Maya take hold of? 13. What did the four Great Brahmas say? 14. What fell from the sky at the birth of the child?

THE BODHISATTVA'S YOUTH

On the seventh day after the birth of Gautama, his mother died, and he was given into the care of his aunt. King Suddhodana hired nurses for the babe, and some fed him, some washed him, some carried him about. A white canopy was carried over the babe day and night. The boy Gautama was called Siddhartha. He became the darling of the people. His voice was sweet and charming like that of the Karavika-bird in the Himalayas.

When King Suddhodana was sitting as judge, he would take the boy on his lap; and soon the boy, carefully considering, was judging the points of the matter according to justice. The people seeing this, said of him: "A Seer, a Seer!"

Siddhartha's childhood passed without illness. He was wise and quick in learning, so that in a few days he would learn what normally took years to learn.

Now King Suddhodana had three palaces built for Siddhartha, one for the rains, one for the winter, and one for the summer. The king adorned them with every kind of pleasurable thing, and Gautama spent the four months of the rainy season in the rain palace, and the four months of the winter season in the winter palace, and four months of the summer season in the summer palace. So he grew to manhood, and it was time he took a wife.

At length the King sent a messenger to the house of Mahanama to deliver this message: "Let your daughter, I pray, marry my son, the Prince Royal."

Mahanama replied, "I fear the Prince Royal has been brought up delicately. He has learned nothing of chivalry, tilting, wrestling, or boxing. How can I wed my child Yasodhara to anyone who knows nothing of these arts?"

The messenger reported this to the King, who thought, "These words, I fear, are true"; and the King sat silent and still. The Bodhisattva, observing this, asked the cause of his father's grief. His father at first told him not to ask, but at last the King told the Prince Royal.

Siddhartha then spoke: "I am ready to compete with all comers. Let the youths of our nation assemble. I will challenge them in all the arts, and every feat of strength and skill."

The King ordered this to be proclaimed throughout the land. On the seventh day all the youths of the nation assembled. First they competed in the art of writing, and the judge chose the Prince as the quickest, neatest, and best writer among them. Then there was an examination in arithmetic, and the victory went to Siddhartha the Prince. Then they competed in all the martial arts, and again the Prince was the winner.

Then Mahanama said, "I have witnessed the Prince's skill. I pray him now to accept my daughter Yasodhara to wife."

The Prince sent Yasodhara every kind of jewel and ornament. He chose the day, and took her to wife in the palace.

Questions (to be answered in writing)

1. When did Siddhartha's mother die? 2. What names are used for the Bodhisattva? 3. What was the child's voice like? 4. How did Siddhartha judge? 5. What did the people call the young judge? 6. What does the word "Seer" mean? 7. How did Siddhartha learn? 8. How many palaces were built for the child? 9. What was the King's message to Mahanama? 10. What was Mahanama's reply to the King? 11. What did Siddhartha tell the King? 12. What was held on the seventh day? 13. What examinations were given? 14. Who won all the competitions? 15. What did Mahanama say after the competitions? 16. What was the name of Mahanama's daughter?

THE FOUR SIGNS

On a certain day the Prince desired to go into the park. He called his charioteer, who yoked the four royal Sindh horses of the color of white lotus petals. Then the charioteer informed the Bodhisattva Siddhartha he had done so. The Bodhisattva got into the chariot, which was like a throne of the gods and went towards the park.

In the park the Siddhartha saw a man infirm with age, broken-toothed, grey-haired, bent, with crooked body, leaning on a staff, trembling. Then the Prince asked the charioteer, "Friend, who is that man? Even his hair is not like that of the others."

The charioteer said it was only an old man, and on hearing his reply the Siddhartha said, "Woe upon birth, since through it old age must come to those who are born." With a troubled heart, he returned and entered the palace.

The King asked, "Why does my son return so quickly?"

The servants said, "Your majesty, he has seen an old man, and he is going to retire from the world."

"Why will you kill me?" cried the King. "Prepare stage-plays for my son quickly; if he obtains happiness, he will not think of retiring from the world."

Then the King prepared a guard, and set them in all directions to the distance of half a league. The guard was to keep the Prince Siddhartha from seeing any unpleasant thing.

Again, on a certain day, the Bodhisattva went to the park. There he saw a diseased man. The Bodhisattva asked in the same way who this might be. When he was told, the prince returned with a troubled heart and entered the palace. The King also inquired as before, and again set a guard; he put them on all sides of the palace to the distance of three-quarters of a league.

Again another day, when going to the park, the Prince saw a dead body. Having asked in the same way, he returned again with troubled heart to the palace. The King again inquired as before, and again he set a guard. He put men on all sides to the distance of one league.

Again on another day, the Siddhartha went to the park. There he saw a hermit carefully and duly dressed.

"Friend, who is this?" he asked the charioteer.

"Your Highness," replied the charioteer, "this is a hermit-sage." And he described a sage's virtues.

The Bodhisattva was delighted with the thought of renunciation, and that day he went on through the park.

Questions (to be answered in writing)

1. Who is the Bodhisattva? 2. Where did the Bodhisattva want to go? 3. What did the charioteer do? 4. Whom did the Bodhisattva see first in the park? 5. What was the Bodhisattva's thought when he saw the old man? 6. What did the King do when the Bodhisattva returned to the palace for the first time? 7. What did the prince see the second time he started for the park? 8. What did the prince do when he was told the man was diseased? 9. What did the prince see the third time he started for the park. 10. Did the prince go through the park the third time? 11. What did the Bodhisattva see the fourth time he set out for the park?

12. What was the prince's reaction to the hermit? 13. What does the word "sage" mean? 14. What is renunciation? 15. What did the prince do the fourth time?

THE GREAT RENUNCIATION

In time King Suddhodana heard that Siddhartha's wife had born a son. The king said, "Announce the happy news to my son."

The Bodhisattva, when he heard, said, "An impediment is born, a fetter is born."

On hearing these words, the King said, "Henceforth let the name of my grandson be prince Rahula." For the word Rahula in Sanskrit means impediment.

Sometime later, the Bodhisattva mounted a splendid chariot, and he entered the city with great honor. Afterwards the Bodhisattva returned to his palace and lay down upon the royal couch. Now beautiful women came round him, entertaining him with dancing, singing, and music; and he fell asleep for a short time.

The women thought, "He for whose sake we are dancing and singing has fallen asleep. Why do we weary ourselves?" Taking their instruments, they strewed them about, and lay down. The Bodhisattva, waking up, saw all these women sleeping with their instruments thrown about. Some of the women were grinding their teeth in their sleep. Some were snoring; some were muttering; some lay with their mouths open. On seeing their disgraceful appearance, the hall seemed to the Bodhisattva like a cemetary filled with all sorts of corpses.

The Bodhisattva then thought, "Today I must make the great renunciation."

He arose from his bed and went towards the door. "Who is there?" he said.

Channa, who had put his head on the threshold, said, "Noble sir, it is I, Channa."

"Today I wish to make the great renunciation. Saddle me a horse."

Channa replied, "Yes, your Highness."

Taking the horse-trappings, Channa went to the stable. He saw Kanthaka, the king of horses standing in a goodly stall.

"This is the one I must saddle today," said Channa and he saddled Kanthaka. The horse, as he was being saddled, thought, "This is a very tight harness. It is not like the harness used on other days in going for pleasure in the park. My noble master must be wishing to make the great renunciation." So with delighted mind, he gave a great neigh.

When the Bodhisattva had sent Channa, he thought, "Now I will go and see my son." He arose from where he was sitting and went to the room of Rahula's mother, and he opened the door. A scented oil-lamp was burning in the room. The mother of Rahula was sleeping on a bed strewn with jasmine and other flowers. Her hand was on her son's head.

The Bodhisattva put his foot on the threshold and stood looking. "If I move the queen's hand and take my son," he said, "the queen will awake. Thus there will be an obstacle in my going. When I have become a Buddha, I will come and see him." And he went down from the palace.

With Channa riding behind him, the Bodhisattva passed through the city gates, and rode as far as the river Anoma. He there crossed the river, and started to send Channa back with the horse.

But the horse Kanthaka, who stood listening to the voice of the Prince as he talked with Channa, thought, "Now I shall never see my master again." When the Bodhisattva passed out of sight, Kanthaka was unable to bear the grief. His heart broke, and he died.

At first Channa had had one grief, but when Kanthaka died, he was overcome by a second grief. He returned weeping and lamenting to the city.

Questions (the answers are to written out in full)

1. What did the Bodhisattva reply when told of the birth of his son? 2. What does the word Rahula mean? 3. What did the entertainers do when the prince dozed off? 4. What did the prince think of when he awoke and saw the entertainers sleeping? 5. What does the word renunciation mean? 6. Whom did the Bodhisattva order to prepare a horse? 7. What was the name of the horse saddled for the Bodhisattva? 8. Why did the Bodhisattva not pick up the baby? 9. Where did the Bodhisattva cut off his hair? 10. What happened to Kanthaka? 11. What were the two sorrows of Channa?

THE PILGRIMAGE

After the charioteer had left to return for Kapilavastu, the prince took his own sword and cut off his hair. He exchanged clothes with an old hunter, and walked on, saying, "This is too near Kapilavastu. I may be disturbed by the Sakyas. I will cross the Ganges and go to Rajagriha." And the prince set out for Rajagriha.

When Prince Siddhartha came into the land of Magadha, Bimbisara, the king, noticed him from a terrace of the palace. King Bimbisara was struck by the noble bearing of the bodhisattva, and the king went to visit him. Bimbisara asked who he was and whence he came. The king offered him riches and position in the land. The bodhisattva replied: "King, I belong to the tribe of the Sakyas in a rich and prosperous country near the Himalayas. I am of the Ksatriya caste. I do not care for this world's treasures. They cannot bring contentment. It is hard to cross the swamps of human passions. They are the roots of fear, of sorrow, of despair. I seek to conquer desires, not to give in to them. The treasure I am seeking is that wisdom which knows no superior."

King Bimbisara then asked, "When you have reached your goal, come back and teach me that unsurpassed wisdom." The bodhisattva then promised that he would, and he went on to the Vulture's Peak near Rajagriha.

At Vulture's Peak the bodhisattva lived with the ascetics who dwelt there. He surpassed them all in their self-tortures, but finally he knew they were not in the right way, and he left these ascetics. He went then from one teacher to another, but they could not answer his questions and he departed thence.

Five other seekers joined him, and they went to the south of Mount Gaya, where the bodhisattva began a new set of self-tortures. Gradually he made these more and more severe. He fasted until he reduced his food to a single grain of rice each day. His body was emaciated and of a blackish-red color.

Finally the bodhisattva saw that this self-torture had not brought him nearer to the truth. He decided then to take some food. When the five brethren saw he took food, they left him. They thought he would never attain to enlightenment. The five brethren then set out for Benares where they lived in the deer-park.

When the bodhisattva had recovered his strength, bathed, and the daughters of a villager brought him food; then he crossed the river, and a grass merchant offered him a hand full of grass. Using this, the bodhisattva made himself a seat at the foot of the bodhi-tree.

Seated beneath the Bodhi tree, the bodhisattva reasoned within himself. He saw the cause of existence, of age, of death, and the way to free oneself of all this trouble. All the causes and effects which bring about existence and its cessation became known to him; and the bodhisattva became enlightened, a Buddha.

After the Buddha had stayed there as long as pleased him, he started out for Benares, journeying along the Nairanjana river.

Questions (to be answered in writing)

1. What did Prince Siddhartha do after the charioteer left?
2. Why did the bodhisattva set out for Rajagriha? 3. Who saw the
bodhisattva when he came to Magadha? 4. What did Bimbisara
offer the bodhisattva? 5. What did the bodhisattva say was his
goal? 6. What did Bimbisara ask the bodhisattva to do? 7. What
did the bodhisattva do after he left Vulture's Peak? 8. Who joined
the Buddha in his search? 9. How did the bodhisattva torture
himself? 10. What happened when the bodhisattva stopped tor-
turing himself? 11. Where did the bodhisattva seat himself? 12.
What happened while the bodhisattva sat beneath the bodhi-tree?
13. Where did the Buddha go after his enlightenment? 14. What
does the word enlightenment mean? 15. What is suffering? 16. What
is the cause of suffering? 17. What is meant by the destruction of
suffering? 18. What path leads to the destruction of suffering?

THE BEGINNING OF PREACHING

Now the Lord gradually came to Benares, to the deer-park
Isipatana, where the five brethren were. The five brethren saw the
Lord coming from afar. They decide among themselves, "This,
friends, is the ascetic Gautama coming. He lives in plenty; he has
given up striving and turned to a life of luxury. We must not
address him, nor rise to greet him, nor take his bowl and robe.
But we shall set a seat for him. If he wishes he may sit down."

As the Lord approached the five brethren, they did not
abide by their agreement. They went to meet the Lord. One took
his bowl and robe. One arranged a seat. One set a footstool, and a
cloth. The Lord sat on the appointed seat. Then they addressed
the Lord by name, and by the title of friend.

When they spoke thus, the Lord said to the five brethren,
"Brethren, do not address the Tathagata by name, nor by the title
of friend. The Tathagata, brethren, is an arahat, and has obtained

complete enlightenment. Give ear, brethren, I have attained the immortal: I instruct, I teach the doctrine. If you walk according to the teaching, for the sake of which noble youths go forth completely from a house to a houseless life, you will soon, on going forth yourselves, realize the highest powers in this life. You will live in the attainment of the aim of the highest religious life."

At these words the five brethren said to the Lord, "Will you, when you live in plenty, have given up trying, and have turned to a life of plenty, now attain supernatural excellence of most noble knowledge and insight?"

The Lord said to the five brethren, "Brethren, the Tathagata does not turn to a life of plenty. The Tathagata, brethren, is an arahat. He has attained complete enlightenment. Give ear, brethren, I have attained the immortal: I instruct, I teach the doctrine. If you walk according to the teaching for the sake of which noble youths go forth completely from a house to a houseless life, you will soon, on going forth yourselves, realize the transcendent faculties in this life. You will live in the attainment of the aim of the highest religious life."

A second and third time the brethren asked the question, and the third time the Buddha replied: "Do you perceive, brethren, that I have never spoken to you thus before now?"

"Never thus, reverend sir."

"The Tathagata, brethren, is an arahat, and has attained complete enlightenment." Then the Lord talked on and was able to convince the five brethren. They listened again to the Lord, gave ear, and fixed their minds on the knowledge.

Then the Lord addressed the five brethren: "Two extremes, brethren, are not to be practiced by one who has given up the world. What are the two? The one, devotion to lusts and pleasures is base, sensual, vulgar, ignoble, and useless. The other practice of self-mortification which is painful, useless and unprofitable. By avoiding these two extremes, brethren, the Tathagata has gained perfect knowledge of the middle path, which produces insight and knowledge. This middle path conduces to tranquility, to transcendent knowledge, to complete enlightenment, to Nirvana.

What is this middle path, brethren? It is the noble Eightfold Path, that is right views, right aspirations, right speech, right action, right livelihood, right endeavour, right mindfulness, and right meditation. This brethren, is the middle path, of which the Tathagata has gained perfect knowledge. This middle path produces insight and knowledge, and leads to tranquility, to supernatural faculty, to complete enlightenment, to Nirvana."

Then the Buddha continued. "This, brethren, is the noble truth of suffering: birth is suffering, old age is suffering, illness is suffering, death is suffering. Union with unpleasant things is suffering; separation from pleasant things is suffering; not obtaining what we wish is suffering, in short the five-fold clinging to existence is suffering. And this, brethren is the noble truth of the cause of suffering: craving, which causes rebirth, accompanied by pleasure and lust, and rejoices at finding delight here and there, that is, craving for pleasure, craving for existence, and craving for prosperity. And this, brethren, is the noble truth of the destruction of suffering: which is the complete and trackless destruction of that thirst, its abandonment and relinquishment, liberation, and aversion. And this, brethren, is the noble truth of the path that leads to the destruction of suffering, that is right views, right mindedness, right speech, right action, right livelihood, right endeavour, right mindfulness, and right concentration."

When the five brethren heard this, they became followers of the Buddha.

Questions (to be answered in writing)

1. Where were the five brethren? 2. What did the five decide among themselves? 3. What did the five do when the Lord approached? 4. What did the Lord tell them he had obtained? 5. How many times did the Lord tell them he had become an arahat? 6. What does the word arahat mean? 7. What two extremes does the Buddha speak of? 8. What does the middle path

produce? 9. What is the middle path an avoidance of? 10. What is another name for the middle path? 11. What are the eight steps of the Eightfold Path?

THE FIVE PRECEPTS

The Buddha Sakyamuni once was teaching his disciples. He spoke of the layman who was not a monk. "A householder's work will I tell you," said the Buddha. "I will tell you how a lay hearer is to act to be a good disciple. For the complete law of the monk cannot be carried out by him who has a family."

"Let him not kill, nor cause any living thing to be killed. Let him not approve of others killing after he himself has stopped hurting all creatures, for both the strong and the weak tremble in this world before death."

Sakyamuni then told of the second rule for lay disciples: "Let the lay disciple not take knowingly anything that is not given him. Let him not cause anyone to take anything, and let him not approve of those that take things. Let him avoid every sort of theft."

The Buddha then spoke of the third rule: "Let the wise man avoid an unchaste life, as a heap of burning coals. Let him live in chastity."

The fourth rule was then spoken of: "Let no man speak falsely to another in the hall of justice or in the public assembly. Let him not cause anyone to speak falsely. Let him not approve those that speak falsely. Let him avoid all sorts of untruth."

The fifth rule or precept was then told by Sakyamuni: "Let the householder who approves my Teaching not give himself in to intoxicating drink. Let the lay disciple not cause others to drink, nor approve of those that drink, for drinks and drugs may lead men to ruin themselves."

Summing up the five precepts which the lay disciple should try always to observe, the Buddha continued: "Let him not kill any living thing. Let him not take what has not been given him. Let him refrain from unchastity. Let him not speak falsely. Let him abstain from intoxicating drinks."

The Buddha concluded, "Let a wise man with a believing mind gladden the assembly of monks with food and drink. Let him make donations according to his ability. Let him dutifully maintain his parents, and let him practice an honorable trade. There are five trades that must not be carried on by a lay disciple. Which are the five? Trade in swords, trade in human beings, trade in flesh, trade in intoxicants, and trade in poisons. These five must not be carried on by a lay disciple."

Questions (to be answered in writing)

1. What does the word layman mean? 2. What does the word householder mean? 3. Can a layman fulfill all the commands for the monk? 4. What is the first precept? 5. May a Buddhist layman approve of killing? 6. What is the second precept? 7. Can a Buddhist layman approve of any kind of theft? 8. What is the third precept? 9. What is the meaning of the word chastity? 10. What is the fourth precept? 11. May a Buddhist layman lie or approve of lying? 12. What is the fifth precept? 13. May a Buddhist layman get drunk? 14. In what does drinking end? 15. Why should drunkenness be avoided? 16. What should the layman do for the monks? 17. How should a lay Buddhist treat his parents? 18. What sort of a trade should a lay Buddhist follow? 19. What five trades must a lay Buddhist not follow?

WHAT OUGHT TO BE DONE

Thus have I heard: Once the Buddha, the World-honored One, dwelling in a pleasant place, spoke unto Ananda:

Ananda, I say expressly that wrong conduct of body, speech, and thought is something that ought not to be done.

From doing what ought not to be done, this is to be expected: Wise men having seen a person's wrong-doing, blame him. An evil report of him goes abroad. He passes away bewildered. On the breaking up of the body after dying, he arises in the Waste, the Bad Bourn, the Downfall.

Ananda, I say expressly that right conduct of body, speech and thought is something that ought to be done. From doing what ought to be done, this advantage is to be expected: The wise, having known a person's right-doing, praise him. A lovely report of him goes abroad. He passes away not bewildered. On the breaking up of the body after dying, he arises in the Good Bourn, the heaven world.

Abandon what is wrong. It is possible to abandon it. Were it not possible to abandon what is wrong. I would not say: Abandon it. But because it is possible, therefore I say: Abandon what is wrong.

Make what is right become. It is possible to make what is right become. Were it not possible to make what is right become, I would not say: Make what is right become. But because it is possible, therefore I say: Make what is right become.

Questions (to be answered in writing)
1. What kinds of wrong conduct should not be done? 2. What are four results of wrong conduct? 3. What are four results of right conduct? 4. What should men do about right?

THE THREE CHARACTERISTICS

When once Sakyamuni Buddha was teaching the Sangha-congregation, he said: "Whether Buddhas arise or not, it remains a fact that all existing things are impermanent. This is a fixed and necessary part of existence. This fact of impermanence a Buddha discovers and masters. When a Buddha has discovered it and mastered this fact, he teaches it. He minutely explains it. He makes it clear that all existing things are impermanent."

Sakyamuni Buddha continued: "Whether Buddhas arise or whether they do not, it remains a fact that all existence is suffering. This is a fixed and necessary part of existence. This fact of suffering a Buddha discovers and masters. When a Buddha has discovered and mastered this fact, he teaches it and publishes it. He makes it clear that all existence is suffering."

Sakyamuni Buddha then concluded: "Whether Buddhas arise or whether they do not arise, it remains a fact that all existing things are soulless or without ego. This is a fixed and necessary part of existence. This fact of soullessness or egolessness a Buddha discovers and masters. He announces, teaches, and proclaims it. He minutely explains it, and he makes it clear that all existing things are soullessness."

Thus the Buddha taught the Sangha-congregation. He explained and proclaimed the three characteristics of existence.

Questions (to be answered in writing)

1. What is one thing that is a fact whether or not there are Buddhas in the world at any time? 2. What kind of a law of existence is this? 3. What does a Buddha do when he discovers this law of existence? 4. What is another law or characteristic of existence? 5. What is the third law or characteristic fact of existence? 6. What is impermanent or transitory? 7. What does transitory mean? 8. What is suffering or sorrow? 9. What is without ego or soul? 10. What does the word ego mean?

BLESSINGS: THE MANGALA-SUTRA

Thus have I heard: Once the Buddha was dwelling near Sravasti, at Jeta Grove, in Anathapindika's Park. Now when the night was far spent a certain deva of wondrous beauty lit up the whole Jeta Grove. He came to the World-Honored One, saluted him and stood aside. So standing, that deva spoke unto the World-Honored One in verse:

> Many devas and many men have thought about
> blessings,
> Longing for goodly things. O tell me the
> greatest of blessing!

The Lord replied:
> Not to follow after fools, but to follow after the
> wise:
> The worship of the worshipful,—this is the
> greatest blessing.

> To dwell in a pleasant spot, to have done good
> deeds in former births;
> To have set oneself in the right path,—this is the
> greatest blessing.

> Much learning and much science, and a discipline
> well learned,
> Yea, and pleasant speech,—this is the greatest
> blessing.

> The support of mother and father, the cherishing
> of child and wife,
> To follow a peaceful livelihood,—this is the
> greatest blessing.

> Giving of alms, the righteous life, to cherish relatives
> and family relations,
> And to do deeds that bring no blame,—this is the
> greatest blessing.

> To cease and to abstain from sin, to shun in-
> toxicants;

And steadfastness in righteousness,—this is the
greatest blessing.

Reverence, humility, content, and gratitude,
To hear the Teachings of the Dharma at proper times,
—this is the greatest blessing.

Patience, the soft answer, the sight of those
controlled,
And pious talk at regular times,—this is the greatest
blessing.

Restraint, the holy life, understanding of the
Four Noble Truths,
Of one's own self to know the Goal,—this is the
greatest blessing.

A heart untouched by world things, a heart
that is not swayed
By sorrow, a heart passionless, secure,—that is
the greatest blessing.

Invincible on every side, they who do these things
On every side they go to bliss,—theirs is the
greatest blessing.

Questions (to be answered in writing)

1. Where was the Mangala-sutra preached? 2. About what
topic did the deva ask questions? 3. In verse one, what is the
highest blessing mentioned? 4. In verse two, what two blessings
lead to the third blessing? 5. In verse three, what is the meaning
of "discipline"? 6. In verse three, to what do learning and discipline lead? 7. What are the three blessings of laymen mentioned
in verse four? 8. What is meant by "giving alms"? 9. Which of the

five precepts is mentioned in verse six? 10. What is the meaning of "humility"? 11. What is the meaning of "restraint"? 12. What is meant by "a heart untouched by worldly things"? 13. What is the meaning of "invincible"? 14. What is the meaning of the word "bliss"?

GOODWILL: THE METTA-SUTRA

Once the World-Honored One, the Buddha, spoke thus:

This must be done by him who is wise to know what is good for him, by him who has grasped the meaning of the Place of Peace.

He must be able and upright and truly straight; he must be gentle of speech and mild, and he must not have any vain conceit of self.

And he should be content, soon satisfied; he should have but few wants; he should be a person of good sense. He should be composed, discreet, not insolent, nor greedy after gifts.

He should do no mean thing for which other men who are wise may scold him.

Let no man deceive another, nor think scorn of him in any way whatever. Let him not in anger or illwill desire another's unhappiness.

Even as a mother, as long as she lives, watches over her child, her only child—even so should one practice an all-embracing mind unto all beings.

And let a man practice a boundless goodwill for all the world, above, below, across, in every way. Let him practice un-hampered goodwill, without ill-feeling or enmity.

Standing or moving, sitting or lying down, let a man practice goodwill. If he is freed from laziness, let a man establish this mindfulness of goodwill. For this is what men call 'the highest state.'

By passing over wrongful view, by walking righteously, a

man should be gifted with insight and conquer greed. Of a truth, such a one shall come no more to birth in any womb.

Questions (to be answered in writing)

1. How should a person speak? 2. What conceit does the good person not have? 3. What seven attitudes should a man have? 4. What should a person not do? 5. How should a man treat another person? 6. What should one practice towards all beings? 7. During what actions should one practice goodwill or loving thoughts? 8. What shall come to such a person?

AUTHORITY IN BUDDHIST TEACHING

Once the Buddha, the World-Honored One, the Well-farer, spoke to Kalamas, saying:

Now look you, Kalamas. Do not be misled by learning in the scriptures. Do not be misled by mere logic and inference, nor after considering arguments. Do not be misled by reflection on some view and approval of it, nor because it fits becoming. Do not be misled because the man who holds a view is your teacher. But when you know for yourselves: These things are not good, these things are faulty; these things are censured by the intelligent; these things, when performed and undertaken, lead to loss and sorrow—then do you reject them.

Questions (to be answered in writing)

1. Should we rely unquestioningly on tradition or hearsay? 2. Should Buddhists blindly rely on learning in the scriptures to prove a point? 3. Is mere logic enough to prove a point? 4. Should a Buddhist blindly accept his teacher's views? 5. On what basis should we reject ideas and actions?

THE LAYMAN'S PROFIT AND LOSS

Once the World-Honored One addressed the laymen of Pataligama:

"There are these five losses, housefathers, which attend the wicked and immoral man. What five?

The wicked immoral man, as the result of laziness, comes to great loss of wealth. That is the first loss.

Then again, evil stories are told about him. That is the second loss.

Then again, whatever company he may enter, be it a company of the nobles, or the Brahmans, or the housefathers or a company of monks, he enters shyly and confused in mind. That is the third loss.

Again, he is troubled in mind when he dies. That is the fourth loss.

And lastly, upon the breakup of the body, after death, he is reborn in the Ill-path, the Downfall, the Place of Suffering.

Such are the five losses that the wicked and immoral man has.

Now there are these five profits, housefathers, that come to the righteous man who lives virtuously:

The righteous man who lives virtuously comes by a great mass of wealth, due to his own work. That is the first profit.

Then again, a good reputation is his. That is the second profit.

Then again, into whatsover company he enters, be it of the nobles, or the Brahmins, or the housefathers, or the recluses—he enters bold and confident. That is the third profit.

Then again, he dies with mind untroubled. That is the fourth profit.

Lastly, on the break-up of body, after death, he is reborn in the Blissful, Happy World. That is the fifth profit.

Such, housefathers, are the five profits that attend the righteous man who lives virtuously."

Questions (to be answered in writing)

1. What does "immoral" mean? 2. What leads to the loss of wealth? 3. What does "attend" mean in this passage? 4. What is the second loss of the evil man? 5. How is the evil man in the company of others? 6. What kind of mind does the evil man have at death? 7. How does an evil man fare at death? 8. What is the meaning of "virtuous"? 9. What kind of a reputation does a virtuous man have? 10. What is the first profit of a virtuous man? 11. How does a virtuous man act in company? 12. What kind of mind does the virtuous man have at death? 13. How does the virtuous man fare at death?

GOOD WORKS

Thus spake the World-Honored One: "Be not afraid of good works, brethren. It is another name for happiness. Good works is another name for what is desired, dear and delightful."

I myself, brethren, have reaped for many a long day the profit of good works. For seven years I once practiced kindly thought, and as a result I came not back into this world for seven kalpas of the unrolling and rolling up of the world. When the kalpa had unrolled, I became one of the splendid Devas. When the kalpa had rolled up, I was reborn in the Highest Abode. I was a Brahma, a great Brahma, the god, the all-seeing Controller.

Thirty and six times, brethren, was I Sakka, Lord of the Devas. Countless hundreds of times was I a rajah, a world ruler, a righteous monarch. I ruled a realm that enjoyed the blessing of security.

Then, brethren, this thought came to me: Of what deeds, I wonder, is all this the fruit? Of what deed is it the ripening, so that I am now thus prosperous and of such mighty power?

Then, brethren, this thought came to me: This is the fruit of three deeds. It is the fruit of the deeds of Charity, Self-taming, and Self-control.

Questions (to be answered in writing)

1. What is another name for good works? 2. For how long had the Buddha once practiced kindly thought? 3. What was the cause of the bodhisattva's becoming the god Brahma? 4. How many times was the bodhisattva king of the gods? 5. What other high offices had the bodhisattva held? 6. What deeds brought these high offices to the bodhisattva?

CONSIDERING RIGHT CONDUCT

Once the Buddha, the World-Honored One, the Arahat, spoke on right and wrong deeds:

Rahula, when you come to want to do any deed of body, speech, or thought, you should reflect: Does it lead to the harm of self, to the harm of others, to the harm of both? Is it wrong? Does it produce ill? Does it result in ill? If you know that it does lead to the harm of self or to the harm of others or to the harm of both and that it is wrong, the, Rahula, as far as you are able, do not do such a deed. You should hold back from it. You should confess it and disclose it, so as to come to control in the future. But should you know, upon reflection, that a deed of body, speech, or thought that you want to do does not lead to the harm of self or to the harm of others or to the harm of both and that it is right, produces of good, is good in result, then a deed such as this is to be done by you. As a result you may go along in joy and delight, training yourself day and night in states that are right.

Questions (to be answered in writing)

1. How should one reflect about any deed? 2. What three kinds of deeds are talked about here? 3. When should you not do a deed? 4. When should you do a deed? 5. What frame of mind does one have when he does a good deed?

THE LAST WORD

Sakyamuni Buddha, when he first set in motion the wheel of righteousness, saved Kondanna. In his last sermon, he saved Subhadra. Those who were to be saved he has saved. Now he lay among the Sal trees, about to enter Nirvana. The time was the middle of the night, calm and noiseless. For the sake of all the disciples, he briefly spoke of the most important doctrines to the monks.

"Brethren! After my death you must reverence and honor the precepts. They are like finding a light in the darkness, like a poor man finding a great treasure. You ought to know, therefore, they are indeed your great teacher. There should be no difference in these, from when I myself lived on earth.

"You ought not tell fortunes, study the stars' positions, or cast horoscopes by the waxing and the waning of the moon. You ought not reckon days of good fortune. All these are things which are improper.

"Control your bodies. Eat at proper times. Conduct yourselves in purity. You should not concern yourselves with worldly matters. Do not circulate rumors, nor recite incantations nor mix potions. Do not bind yourselves to eminent people in friendship nor become familiar with them that you can boast of it indecently. All these are not to be done! You ought, with fixed mind, in Right Mindfulness, aspire to liberation. You ought not conceal your faults. Do not give rise to heresy, nor lead people astray.

"I shall speak briefly about the forms for protecting the precepts. The precepts are the basis of the decision of release. If you rely on the cause from the precepts, you will attain many stages of concentration and the knowledge of the extinction from suffering. Therefore, you ought always keep the precepts pure and never break them. If man can hold these precepts pure, this indeed will be good. If there are no pure precepts, no good merit can arise at all.

"Brethren! If you want to live the precepts, you must control the five senses. Their five desires must not enter through your neglect. It is just like a cowherd, taking a stick and by showing it, stops the cows from entering another man's field which is ripe for the harvest. So, if you indulge the five senses, their desires not be stopped within bounds. You will be subject to pain through many kalpas: your whole existence will be suffering. The evil of that robber (the five senses) extends through many lives, creating very great pain. For this reason, wise men control the senses. These desires should be kept like prisoners who may not wander about. As for these five senses, the mind acts as their master. For this reason you must always guard your mind well. Life, for example, is like a man who carrying some honey, goes bouncing along his path looking only at the honey and fails to notice a deep hole. Hasten to turn aside your desires. If you indulge this mind, you lose the good of being a man. If you limit desires, there is nothing you cannot accomplish. For this reason, brethren, you ought to strive diligently and subdue your minds.

"Brethren: In receiving all food and drink you ought to accept them as medicine. You must not accept or reject what you like or dislike: just support your bodies and avoid starvation and thirst. Accept just enough of peoples' offerings to avoid distress! Don't have many demands and thereby break peoples' good hearts. A wise man, for example, having judged the amount of capacity of his ox's strength, does not wear out its strength by overloading.

"Brethren! Don't waste your time! In the early evening, nor even late at night, do not cease your struggle. Even in the middle of the night, you should inform yourselves better by reading the sutras. You will gain nothing by passing your whole life in vain through sleep. You ought to think of the world as burning in a fire. You must desire to save yourself quickly. You must not sleep! Depravities are a poison.

"The clothing of conscience, among all finery, is the very best. Conscience is like an iron goad which can control man's righteousness. Therefore, brethren, you must always be conscientious. You must not be able, even for a moment, to ignore it.

If you depart from conscience, you lose all merit. He who has regrets has that which is good. He who has no regrets will not be different from birds or beasts.

"Brethren! If there were a man who came and dismembered you joint by joint, you should not hate him, but rather include him in your heart. And you must guard your mind that no complaining word come out of it. If you give way to hateful thoughts, there is a barrier in your own way, and you lose the benefit of your merit. Patience is a virtue which the keeping of every precept or any other austerity cannot equal. He who can practice patience can truly be called the great and strong man. He who cannot endure abuse as he would drink a sweet drink cannot be called an enterer of the way or a wise man. Why is that? Because the harm of hatefulness shatters all good. It destroys your good name so that, in present or future generations, man will not wish to see it. You should realize that hateful thoughts are worse than a great fire. You must always guard and watch yourselves. Do not let hate gain entrance. No robber steals your merit more than hatefulness. Those householders, dressed in white, who have desires and do not practice the way, are not in righteous control of themselves. Even hatred is understandable in them. But, just as lightning and thunder cannot appear in a white filmy cloud, it cannot be in the homeless ones who practice the way without desires and control their hatefulness.

"If arrogance and pride arise, you must rapidly extinguish them. The growth of arrogance and pride is not good even for those wearing white and living in the world, much less to say for the homeless ones who, having entered the way to achieve release, subdue their bodies and practice begging.

"Brethren! A mind full of flattery is not suited to the way. Therefore, you must in simplicity correct such a mind. You must understand that flattery is only cheating. The man who has entered the way, therefore, has no use of flattery.

"Brethren! You must understand that the man of many desires, by reason of his desire for reward, has much suffering too. The man of few desires neither desiring anything nor seeking anything, thereby does not have these sorrows. You ought to practice having only a few desires. The man of few desires need not by flattery sway another's mind, nor is he led by his passions. The man who has few desires has a contented mind. He has no cause for sorrow and fear.

"Brethren! If you want to escape from all suffering, you must see what contentment is. The basis of contentment is, indeed, to obtain rich joy, calmness and peace. The man of contentment, even though he lies on the ground, is still happy. He who is not contented, though he were in heavenly palaces, still would not be connected. He who is not contented, even though he be rich, he is poor. The man who is contented, even though he be poor, is rich. He who is not contented is pulled by the five desires and therefore he is pitied by the one who is contented. This is what is called contentment.

"Brethren! If you desire quietude, inaction, and joy, always avoid confusion and noise. Live alone in a quiet retreat. The man who lives in solitude is respectfully worshipped by Indra and all the gods. Those who rejoice in company have the pains of company, just as when many birds flock upon a great tree, it is in danger of collapse. Attachment to the world drowns one in suffering of mankind, just as an old elephant drowning in the mud cannot get himself out.

"Brethren! If you strive energetically there is nothing that is hard. For example, a constant trickle of water will bore a hole in a rock. Therefore, you must always strive energetically. If the mind of a disciple becomes in many ways idle and inattentive, it is just like making a fire by friction and you rest before it is hot: even if you desire fire, you cannot get a blaze.

"Seek a personal-teacher: Seek a good-friend. There is nothing like not forgetting. If one does not forget, that robber, the depravities, cannot enter. For this reason ye must always have concentration present in your mind. If you lose concentration, you lose all merit thereby. If then your power of concentration is strong and hard, even though the five desires were to enter, they cannot do any harm, just as if you have put on armour to enter the battle, there is nought to fear.

"Brethren! If you unify your mind, your mind is then in concentration. Because your mind is in concentration, you can know the basic nature of the appearance and disappearance of the world. For this reason you must always strive diligently to practice various stages of concentration. If you attain concentration, the mind doesn't wander. Just as a house with little water carefully conserves that in its reservoir, so should the disciple also. For the sake of the water of knowledge you should practice concentration. Do not let it leak away.

"Brethren! If you have perfect knowledge, then you have no greed. Always examine yourself that you do not let yourself be in error. Thereby then, from within subjectivity and objectivity, you can get release. If you do not do so, you already are not a follower of the way, nor are you a white-clad layman either! There would be no suitable name for you. Perfect knowledge is a strong ship which carries you across the sea of old age, sickness and death. Again, it is a great brilliant light in deep darkness. It is a good medicine for all who are ill. It is a sharp ax which cuts the reed of evil. For this reason, you must, by listening, pondering, and practicing knowledge, make yourself progress.

"Brethren! If you enter into many kinds of useless discussion, then your mind will be confused, and, though you leave your homes, still you won't attain release. For this reason, you ought immediately to cease confused thinking and useless discussion.

"Brethren! In all kinds of virtue you must always wholeheartedly get rid of laxity, just as you would a hateful robber. That which the Lord of great compassion has preached for your benefit is now concluded. Yet you must strive diligently to practice it. Whether you live in the mountains or in the lowlands, whether you live under a tree or in seclusion in a quiet room, ponder the doctrines which you have received. You must not let them become lost. You must always exert yourself to practice them energetically. If you do not do this and die vainly, afterwards it will be the occasion of much regret. I am like a good doctor, who recognizes the illness and prescribes a medicine: but whether it will actually be taken or not is up to the doctor. Again, I am like a good guide who directs a man to the best path. If, on hearing that, he doesn't go on it, the fault is not with the guide.

"Brethren! If you have any doubts regarding the Four Truths, you ought to ask about them immediately. You must not have concealed doubts without wishing to dispel them." At that time, the Lord spoke thus three times, but there was no man who questioned him. What was the reason? Because the assembly had no doubts! At that time Aniruddha, seeing what was in the minds of those assembled, said to the Buddha: Lord! The moon might grow hot, and the sun might grow cool, but the four truths which Buddha taught, is of real suffering which cannot become joy. Accumulation of desires truly is its cause, and there can never be a different cause. If suffering is destroyed, it is when its cause had been destroyed. If the cause is destroyed, its result is destroyed. The way of destroying error is the path of truth, and there is no other path. All these brethren are firm and without doubts concerning the four truths.

"If, in this assembly there are those who have not finished their task, perhaps on seeing the passing of the Buddha they shall feel sad. If there are any who has just entered the way, on hearing what the Buddha is teaching, he will attain salvation. As clearly as one sees lightening in the night, he then can see the way. If anyone has already finished his task and already has crossed the sea of suffering, he will think only this: 'The Lord has passed on. Why was this done so rapidly?'" Although Aniruddha had spoken these words, all, without exception, in the assembly clearly penetrated the meaning of the four holy truths, the Lord wished all in this great assembly might become stronger. With a mind of great compassion, he spoke for the benefit of the assembly.

"Brethren! Don't feel grieved! If I were to live in the world a whole kalpa, our association would still have to end. You cannot find any association which does not end. The doctrine of benefit to one and all has been completed. If I were to live longer, it would be of no benefit. Those who were to be saved in both heaven and earth, have all without exception been saved. Those who have not been saved, have all, again, created the cause of their attaining salvation. From now on, all my disciples, turning it over in their minds, must practice this; thereby this will be the Body of the Tathagata's Law, which will be forever without destruction.

"Therefore you must know the world is all transient, and meeting certainly implies separation. Don't feel grieved! Such is the nature of the world. You must strive diligently and seek immediate release. With the light of perfect knowledge, destroy all the darkness of ignorance. The world is dangerous and perishable, and there is nothing strong and enduring. Now I attain extinction: this is like getting rid of a bad sickness. This, which we call a body, is a criminal thing. It is sunk in the great ocean of birth and death. Is there a wise man who would not be glad to get rid of this, like one might kill a hateful robber?"

"Brethren! You ought always aspire wholeheartedly to the way of release. The whole world of moving and non-moving forms is in appearance disquieting and not calm. Stop a moment! Speak not! Time is passing away. I am going to nirvana. This is what I have taught at the last."

Questions (to be answered in writing)

1. Between what trees did the Buddha die? 2. Whom did he save in his last sermon? 3. What are the commandments like? 4. What is to be the teacher of the brotherhood when the Buddha is gone? 5. Are the monks to concern themselves with worldly matters? 6. What is the result of indulging the five senses? 7. What is the finest clothing? 8. What should a monk do to a person who kills him and cuts up his body? 9. What is to be done to arrogance

and pride? 10. What does the man of few desires have? 11. Where ought a monk live who desires quietude? 12. When can the depravities not enter? 13. What does the word depravity mean? 14. What is perfect knowledge likened to? 15. In what way is the Buddha like a doctor? 16. How long will the Four Noble Truths be true? 17. What is to be the Body of the Tathagata's Law?

APPENDIX A BUDDHIST SANGHA AWARD INFORMATION

THE PURPOSE

The purpose of the Sangha Award is to give the Buddhist Scouts a practical guidance in achieving the spiritual pledge made in the Scout Oath and Law, thereby developing a boy whose views and actions in life would stem from the highest of the Buddhist thoughts.

The Sangha Award program aims to do this by leading the boy: 1) to attain understanding and faith in the Buddha, 2) to learn the Teachings, and 3) to practice the harmonious Buddhist way of life, in the spirit of universal brotherhood of all living things. These are the dynamic aspects of the boy's complete acceptance of the Three Treasures (Buddha, Dharma, and Sangha).

Further, the Award program duly recognizes the twelfth point of the Scout Law that the scout "is faithful in his religious duties and respects the convictions of others in matters of custom and religion." The scout is expected to receive religious training and participate actively in his temple program.

Finally the Sangha Award program gives the scout a solid basis for fuller understanding and a greater appreciation of all phases of the scouting program.

THE AWARD AND
WHAT IT MEANS

The Sangha Award is a medal consisting of a pendant, ribbon, and a bar. The pendant is the Wheel of Dharma, sometimes called the Wheel of Life. It is a symbol which represents the spreading of Buddha's Teachings. The Wheel is suspended from a multi-colored ribbon representing the aura of Buddha's many virtues. This ribbon is attached to a crossbar in which is inscribed the Sanskrit word, "Sangha," meaning brotherhood.

The Boy Scouts of America has authorized the Sangha Award to be worn on the Official Uniform over the left breast pocket, to the left of the Eagle Badge, or, when the Eagle Badge is not worn, centered above the flap of the left breast pocket.

The Award is presented by the temple to a Buddhist Scout in recognition of his spiritual growth as shown by his fulfilling the Award requirements.

The requirements are made quite flexible to suit different conditions, so that any Buddhist Scout who sincerely and earnestly applies himself to meeting the requirements of this Award will find it to be very rewarding.

WHO IS ELIGIBLE?

Any Buddhist boy who is a registered member of a Scout Troup or Explorer unit may apply and begin qualifying for the Sangha Award. Since this is an individual program, a Buddhist Scout who is a member of any unit may qualify whether or not his unit is sponsored by a Buddhist temple. A boy can start at any rank in scouting, but in order to receive the Award he must be at least a First Class, and an Explorer must have had at least one year in exploring.

HOW TO EARN THE AWARD

1. Send for an application form by writing to the National Buddhist Committee on Scouting.

2. Mail the application form together with a one dollar registration fee. On approval of your application, you will receive a Service Record Book and a suggested list of study materials.

3. Begin your study under close guidance of your minister or a counselor appointed by your minister.

4. After you have fulfilled all the requirements of stage one satisfactorily, have your minister write a letter of certification and you will be given a certificate.

5. After fulfilling all the requirements for the Sangha Award to the satisfaction of your minister or counselor, arrangements will be made for you to appear before the Sangha Award Board of Review.

6. If the Sangha Award Board of Review finds that you have maintained the high standard set for the requirements, your Record Book will be certified, and with a letter of certification, sent to the National Buddhist Committee on Scouting for final approval.

7. When all approval is made, a Sangha Award will be forwarded to the minister of your temple to be presented to you at an appropriate ceremony.

ADMINISTRATION

The Sangha Award program is administered and supervised by the National Buddhist Committee on Scouting. However, the Boy Scouts of America through its National Regional, and District Councils is giving full support and encouragement to this program. The scout leaders are acquainted with the church award program.

For further information contact your local Buddhist temple, your local Scout Executive, or the National Buddhist Committee on Scouting whose address is below.

NATIONAL BUDDHIST COMMITTEE ON SCOUTING
c/o BUDDHIST CHURCHES OF AMERICA
1710 Octavia Street
San Francisco, California 94109

Hawaii Area Office:
1727 Pali Highway
Honolulu, Hawaii 96813

APPENDIX B REQUIREMENTS FOR THE AWARD

FIRST STAGE

BUDDHA

1. Relate briefly the life of Sakyamuni Buddha and name about five principal events of His life, their dates, and point out on a map where they occurred.

2. Explain what is meant by a Buddha.

3. Explain in your own words what Buddha means to you in your personal life.

4. Show that you have provided the necessary daily care of the shrine in your home for at least three months.

5. Demonstrate the correct method of shrine arrangement.

6. Show evidence of personal daily morning and evening meditation before the shrine.

7. Explain and demonstrate correct etiquette and procedures before the shrine, including gassho, use of meditation beads (juzu), incense burning, etc.; and give the symbolic significance of each.

DHARMA

8. Explain briefly some of the principal teachings of Buddhism and answer the following:
   (a) What are the Four Noble Truths? Noble Eightfold Path?
   (b) What are the three characteristics of existence?

(c) Explain what Buddhist Karma means.

(d) What are the eight sufferings? The ten evils? The six paramitas? The five precepts?

9. State briefly the history of the founder and the development of your own denomination.

SANGHA

10. Show that you, express Buddhist gratitude regularly before and after meals.

11. Describe the administration, the organization, and the affiliated organizations of your own local temple.

12. Show that you attend Sunday School services regularly.

13. Choice of one:
    (A) Plan and complete a project satisfactory to the minister or qualified counselor.
    (B) Give twenty-five hours of dana to your temple by any of the following methods:
    a. Distribution of temple literature, posters, etc.
    b. Collection of articles, etc. for the needy.
    c. Doing errands.
    d. Repairing temple property, decorating rooms.
    e. Cleaning yard, helping in the kitchen, etc.
    f. Clerical services.
    g. Others recommended by the minister or qualified counselor.

15. Know the major acitivities and the events of your temple for the year.

16. Name some of the social welfare activities of your temple and show how you had helped in one or more of them.

SECOND STAGE

BUDDHA

1. Relate the life of Sakyamuni Buddha including the background of His time, the spiritual significance of the various events which led to His enlightenment.

2. Explain Buddha-nature and why there could be many Buddhas.

3. Give the meaning of your shrine symbol.

4. Reach an understanding with your minister or qualified counselor on "Faith."

5. Relate briefly the significance and development of the use of the shrine in Buddhist services.

6. Give the meaning of the historic Buddhist symbols.

7. Lead a family service at home for at least seven different times in three months, using Ti-Sarana (Three Treasures) and any of the following: A sutra of your temple, readings from Dhammapada, passages from the Sunday School text or Young Buddhist Association Service text, or similar text.

DHARMA

8. Explain the following:
   (a) The aim of Buddha's teachings.
   (b) Enlightenment of Nirvana
   (c) The Buddhist concept of self
   (d) Rebirth

9. Explain briefly the characteristics of Theravada and Mahayana Buddhism.

10. Explain the three aspects of Buddha (Trikaya).

11. Name the sutras used in your temple, and give a brief explanation of the sutras and the fundamental teachings on which your temple is based.

12. Exemplify in your daily living the practice of the Noble Eightfold Path, the six paramitas, and the five precepts in the light of the principal beliefs of your temple.

SANGHA

13. Give the meaning and relate the history of the Buddhist Sangha.

14. Show that you are giving financial contributions regularly to your temple, as well as attending your temple and/or Y.B.A. services.

15. Know the history and the administrative organization of your temple system in our country, and include the counterpart of your temple in some foreign country.

16. Explain one or more of your temple's foreign welfare services, and show how you have participated in it.

17. Show active participation in the youth organization of your own temple.

18. Show ability and willingness to do any one of the following:
    (a) Lead a Y.B.A. service, Sunday School, or choir.
    (b) Be on the Sunday School teaching staff.
    (c) Serve as leading officer of the youth organization.
    (d) Work as conference committee chairman.
    (e) Any other recommended by the minister or qualified counselor.

20. Describe a few of the present worldwide Buddhist movements.

21. As a Buddhist, show how through your own daily living you can contribute toward the achievement of harmony among mankind.